100 WAYS TO EARN

TONY DRAKE

Contents

There is a quote that suggests we all have three currencies, and those currencies are Time, Knowledge, and Money, therefore, any one of the currencies that you lack, use the other two to obtain the one that is absent in your life.

However, what if you lack two or more currencies?

The answer to this question is to prioritize the goal that will produce the results which will enable you to obtain the desired results to then accomplish other goals by creating a blueprint or template for success going forward which can be applied to any goal, as success seeds success.

To simplify this equation let us assume that you lack money and time both of which you need to obtain your IT Certification, because you work every day having little time to study yet do not earn enough to complete your certification as living expenses consume ninety percent of your income.

A Practical approach to this problem would be to save a percentage of your income weekly or monthly to achieve the following results, One, buy back a percentage of your time to study through your savings, even if you have to work two or more jobs for a time, enough savings through working within your capacities must accumulate adequate savings to both buy back your time and pay for your certification.

The process may be difficult in many ways; however, discipline and time management will produce the results that you desire, therefore it is critical that you concentrate all of your efforts and determination towards this goal while eliminating Clutter, Options, Distractions, and Excuses, from this level of commitment success is surely yours.

Now that you understand the three currencies and how to use them, add one more currency to the Money category, the addition is cryptocurrencies and the blockchain which offers unlimited digital asset opportunities available to increase the value, potential, and scalability of the three Currencies.

Here is the key lesson that you will derive value from if you are willing to implement this truth as quickly as you can in your life to both secure and enhance the quality of your life for many years to come.

The lesson is composed of four columns that will support the structure of your life's foundation in which you may continue to build upon indefinitely, learn the language and real purpose of money, this knowledge will assist you in working for assets instead of money, appropriate allocated assets will then generate income for you so that you will not have to work for money.

The second lesson is to value your time, as time is your very life, the more of it that you give away working for others the less time you will have for yourself to live the life that you imagine that you could have, and always keep this in mind, that your time is your fortune when used wisely to obtain and apply the appropriate knowledge of money, technology as it relates to money and various assets which may be digital or tangibles. Assets make life better when utilized based upon sound uncommon knowledge.

Lesson three is the power of mind, to control your thoughts, emotions, desires, and your will power is both critical and essential in order to power push your way into any success that you prioritize. The power of inner vision to see within your abilities that others cannot see is visualized mind power on a mission of manifestation, imagine the times that you thought of something so intensely that it manifested itself, to bring your visions into reality requires that you control what goes into your mind and how you cultivate and manage the value of substance that you enter into your mind.

Never allow garbage or disruptive events to enter into your mind, such circumstances are only there to steal and capture your attention to feed its purpose whatever that might be.

Keep your mind and thoughts clean at all times, if this requires that you shut out all forms of media and related sources of mass information mediums, then do it, protect your peace of mind through cleanliness and the sanctity harnessed in the power of your mind.

The more that you learn of that which offer and provide value to the world will always increase exponentially your abilities to earn income at scale even when you are no longer in this world, so continue to increase your learning while applying what you have learned, you will remain wealthy and healthy all of the days of your life.

Now the final lesson here, incapsulates all four lessons into a single mindset of success in all things, and that is freedom, learning the language of money, assets that generate income, enhanced by the control and command of your own mind forged by will power becomes the enduring fire wall for freedom from all forms of bondage, debt, BS, bad relationships, and unwanted chaos and misery in the life that you have forged from good substance and mind to form your vision through imagination, visualization, and constant affirmations through mind and work.

These lessons constitute the finest qualities of life, now you must adapt and apply these lessons right now to save yourself from the miseries and sufferings of not acquiring these life lessons. The secret to happiness is freedom and the secret to freedom is courage, act consistently and improve your knowledge through action to improve your results through continuous learning.

Let us now explore not only the three currencies that can solve everyday problems through the Blockchain including over one hundred ways to generate income through the combination of social media, Ai, and the blockchain.

The integrated system presented in this work will forever change how you see income, assets, intellectual property, commodities, labor and Debt, this we promise you, now let us get started.

There are three levels of earning income legally:

1) Money and Power Supported by Strong Contacts and Connections
2) Intellect with marketable in demand skills backed by experience
3) Labor or trading time for money

This where we begin this journey of clarity to forge a path of freedom through liberation of the mind, body, soul and spirit.
Thank You in advance for choosing this publication to acquire more knowledge to increase your wellbeing on this life's journey of expanding change.

Opened Eyes

Opened eyes can never be closed once exposed to light, exposure to the light of facts and uncommon knowledge compels one to seek further into all of its intricacies, and sometimes the search for more information can become an obsession of sorts, however, if that information is not being applied in real time towards an objective, then there is a natural law of use that comes into play.

And that law is exercise or that which is used become stronger vs, that which is not used become weaker over time, information applied becomes knowledge, when practiced and applied over and over again becomes experienced, then a professional and expert. So, use everything that is presented in this publication to firmly establish the control and foundational command of your time, mind, money, and freedom.

In the first chapter of this publication, give your full attention to the progressive steps provided which leads successively to the next set of actions presented in the following chapter as it will present each key chapter of information in bite size action assignments, there are five chapters in total which comprise specific tasks to be initiated as an organized step-by-step guide to achieve real results.

The results and experience that you will receive are all invaluable skills that you may continue to build upon throughout your learning process, there is always more to learn and adopt, therefore keep learning and keep growing, it is the only way to remain relevant in an ever-changing economic-financial landscape.

Chapter One

Blockchain-Ai-Information Technology- M2-20-Social Media Integration Factor

The blockchain is designed to transport messages over a network ledger which cannot be altered via its inherent cryptographic security layers but can also be used to manage all types of data with a speed ratio of transmittal within seconds.

Ai or artificial intelligence is a field of science that build, designs and program machines to behave and function much like a human would without the need for human management.

The M2-20 is a Portable yet powerful blockchain asset generator composed of two mining devices that mines cryptocurrencies with less power and down time.

Social Media is comprised of websites and applications that enable users to create and share content or to participate in social networking.

The combination of these four tools create unlimited opportunities throughout the traditional asset classes to include: Cash, Cash equivalents such as cryptocurrencies, Short-term deposits, Accounts receivables, Inventory, Marketable securities, Office supplies and Precious Metals.

Consider the possibilities of interoperable value transactions of unlimited scale that the Blockchain, Ai, M2-20 asset generator and social media combination impact through an integrated exchange with all current asset classes will have on your investment portfolio.

These combined resource factors are universal in scale but not necessarily uniform, however, sound knowledge and use of these tools offer a pathway to mind mastery, wealth, complete ownership of your time, and unbridled freedom, in whole or part, these attributes are what all humans need and desire in their individual and collective lives; and our full intention is to provide practical steps to achieve real results in this direction.

How to obtain the greatest advantage

It is often more practical and rewarding to focus on integrating high-demand careers and professions across multiple industries rather than limiting oneself to a single sector. By casting a wider net over various high-growth fields, individuals can gain a clearer and more comprehensive view of the opportunities available.

This approach not only helps job seekers and professionals identify positions that align with their interests and goals but also increases their chances of securing roles that offer long-term growth, stability, and personal fulfillment. The dynamic nature of today's job market makes it crucial to adapt by understanding and targeting industries that are consistently expanding and in need of skilled talent.

Our preferred strategy emphasizes the value of combining opportunities from multiple high-demand sectors to unlock greater potential. Instead of relying solely on one career path, we advocate for the intentional acquisition of diverse, yet complementary skill sets that span several thriving industries. This not only increases versatility and marketability but also enables individuals to create unique career portfolios that can open doors to innovation, entrepreneurship, and career advancement. By adopting this multi-industry approach, individuals position themselves to remain competitive, adaptable, and in control of their professional development in an ever-evolving global economy.

Rust Developer – Overview

A Rust Developer is a software engineer who specializes in building high-performance, memory-safe, and concurrent systems using the Rust programming language. Rust is known for its strong safety guarantees, zero-cost abstractions, and efficient handling of system resources without a garbage collector.

Core Responsibilities
- Develop system-level software such as operating systems, embedded systems, game engines, and blockchain technologies.
- Write safe and efficient code using Rust's strict compiler checks to prevent memory leaks, race conditions, and undefined behavior.
- Optimize performance in resource-constrained environments.
- Build concurrent and parallel programs with confidence, leveraging Rust's powerful concurrency model.
- Collaborate with teams using modern development workflows including Git, CI/CD, and code reviews.

Skills Required
- Proficiency in Rust programming and its standard library.
- Solid understanding of memory management, ownership, and borrowing rules.
- Familiarity with systems programming concepts, such as low-level hardware interaction, multithreading, and performance tuning.
- Experience with Cargo, Rust's package manager and build system.
- Knowledge of FFI (Foreign Function Interface) to integrate Rust with other languages like C/C++.

Common Applications

- Blockchain development (e.g., Solana, Polkadot)
- Game engines and game development
- Embedded systems and IoT
- Operating systems and low-level tools
- WebAssembly applications

Why Rust?

Rust is favored for its:

- Memory safety without garbage collection
- Concurrency without data races
- Modern tooling and growing ecosystem
- Strong compile-time guarantees
- Foundational Level (Beginner) Time Line- three hours per day five day per week, eight weeks total, hours committed #120, now ready for certification testing:

- Focus: Understanding basic concepts, terminology, and principles.
- Activities: Reading textbooks, watching introductory videos, taking beginner-level courses.
- Goal: Build a solid base of knowledge to support further learning.

- Intermediate Level Time Line- five hours per day five day per week, six weeks hours committed #150, now ready for certification testing

- Focus: Applying knowledge, analyzing information, and exploring specialized topics.
- Activities: Case studies, lab work, group discussions, intermediate courses.
- Goal: Develop critical thinking and problem-solving skills in the subject area.

- Advanced Level Time Line- eight hours per day five day per week, 4 weeks hours committed #160, now ready for certification testing

- Focus: Conducting original research, synthesizing complex information, contributing new insights.
- Activities: Writing research papers, conducting experiments, presenting at conferences.
- Goal: Achieve subject mastery and generate new knowledge or innovations

Salary: $150,000 to $180,000

Foundational Strategies for Transitioning into a New Career

Step one: Review the entire course to gain basic insight, at this stage you will not take notes, just review the entire course concentrating your focus on the content only.

Step two: Review the course for two purposes, take notes on the terminology and take notes on every area you do not understand then find the correct way to apply what you have learned through practice exams.

Step three: review all of your notes for clarity and clear understanding of all of the concepts and applications of the new skills which you are learning in the form of creating applications for various functions, this will insure that you are familiar with key concepts.

Step four: It is recommended that you complete the practice examinations, and upon consistently achieving a score of 80% or higher, you will be considered adequately prepared to undertake the final certification examination.

As each new skill set necessitates a distinct timeline for acquisition, the expected duration for completing the learning process will be clearly specified. The foundational learning framework will adhere to the prescribed guidelines to ensure a coherent and methodical progression.

Here are several effective strategies to prepare for and sustain your learning both before rand throughout the learning process:

10 Smart Strategies for Supercharged Focus and Academic Excellence

1. **Fuel Your Brain with Proper Nutrition**
    Maintain a balanced, nutrient-rich diet and stay consistently hydrated with clean water to support cognitive performance and sustained energy levels.

2. **Prioritize Restorative Sleep**
    Ensure 7–9 hours of quality sleep each night to allow your brain to recover, consolidate learning, and stay alert during the day.

3. **Leverage Morning Brainpower**
    Begin studying early in the morning when mental clarity and focus are typically at their highest, making it easier to absorb and retain information.

4. **Study in Structured Blocks**
    Adopt the 2–3 hour study block method with a 15-minute break between sessions to maintain concentration and prevent burnout.

5. **Try Natural Cognitive Enhancers**
    Consider safe and effective supplements like *NeuroGum Energy Caffeine Gum* to boost focus and alertness without overreliance on stimulants.

6. **Declutter Your Environment**
    Create a clean, organized study space free from visual and digital distractions to encourage deep focus and a calm mindset.

7. **Cut Out Mental Noise**
    Eliminate excessive choices, distractions, and excuses that drain willpower and lead to procrastination—streamline your environment and schedule.

  TONY DRAKE

8. **Master the Art of Discipline**

    Cultivate self-discipline by setting clear boundaries, sticking to your study schedule, and holding yourself accountable daily.

9. **Define Your Vision and Purpose**

    Keep a vivid image of your goal in mind—whether it's passing an exam, earning a degree, or mastering a subject—to fuel your motivation and commitment.

10. **Balance Productivity with Self-Care**

    Incorporate daily movement, relaxation techniques, and moments of joy to reduce stress and maintain a healthy, sustainable study-life balance.

Following the roadmap

How we will begin this exciting path to certification success:

- Firstly, all of the professions contain the title, description, learning parameters, salary and learning timelines required to obtain certification.
- Next to each title are several numbers which are direct links to the courses that you will need access to
- Further details pertaining to each profession is provided in this bundle audiobook for enhanced support as well as the course that guides you through every detail for your certification success

Acquiring a new set of high-demand skills can be challenging, but leveraging the comprehensive bundle of tools as your guide can boost your determination to succeed by up to 75%. The three distinguishing factors that make this bundle so effective are the following facts

- ✓ The **eBook** provide details of each professional position and learning parameters, in-depth explanations, research, case studies, diagrams, worksheets, actionable step, links to resource
- ✓ The **audiobook** provides users with deeper insights, key take aways, unconventional strategies that encourage deeper dives into career building based upon uniquely designed income models, listen on the go and more
- ✓ The **course** provide visuals of the process which includes screen recordings, practical implementation and walk throughs designed to maximize your learning experience.
- ✓ There are also levels of engagement taking into consideration that each person has different time lines in which they can commit to

✓ Also to create a viable support network for all users, a membership site is also available to all users so that they may access more tools, resources, and live events on the latest updates on all industries and opportunities available worldwide.

1 AWS Security Specialist 1. 2. 3.

An AWS Security Specialist is a professional who focuses on protecting cloud-based systems, data, and applications that run on Amazon Web Services (AWS). Their primary job is to secure the cloud infrastructure and make sure it complies with best practices, legal regulations, and industry standards.

What Do They Do?
Here are the key responsibilities of an AWS Security Specialist:

Identity and Access Management (IAM):
Set up and manage who can access what in an AWS environment.

Data Protection:
Use tools like AWS KMS (Key Management Service) and encryption to protect sensitive data at rest and in transit.

Network Security:
Configure Virtual Private Clouds (VPCs), security groups, firewalls, and VPNs to protect networks.

Monitoring and Logging:
Use services like AWS CloudTrail, Amazon Guard Duty, and AWS Security Hub to detect threats and monitor suspicious activity.

Compliance & Governance:
Ensure that AWS infrastructure meets standards like GDPR, HIPAA, or ISO 27001. Use AWS Config and AWS Audit Manager.

Incident Response:
Prepare for and respond to security incidents like unauthorized access or data breaches.

Risk Assessment:
Continuously analyze the AWS setup for vulnerabilities and recommend ways to reduce risks.

Tools & Services Commonly Used
AWS IAM – Controls user permissions

Amazon VPC – Secures networking

AWS WAF – Web Application Firewall
Amazon GuardDuty – Threat detection

AWS Config – Configuration compliance

AWS CloudTrail – Logs API activities

AWS Shield – Protects against DDoS attacks

Common Background & Skills
Deep understanding of AWS architecture and services

Knowledge of cybersecurity principles

Familiarity with compliance standards
(like PCI-DSS, NIST)

Experience with cloud automation (using tools like Terraform or CloudFormation)

Certifications (Optional but Valuable)
AWS Certified Security – Specialty

AWS Certified Solutions Architect – Associate/Professional

Certified Information Systems Security Professional (CISSP)

Salary: $53,000 to $115,000 annually with average of $78,000

Engagement Levels to Consider

1. **Foundational Level** (Beginner)

Time Commitment:

- Schedule: 3 hours/day, 5 days/week
- Duration: 8–12 weeks
- Total Hours: ~120 (including test exams)
- Outcome: Prepared for initial certification testing

Focus:

- Grasping fundamental concepts, terminology, and core principles of the subject.

Key Activities:

- Reading foundational textbooks and articles
- Watching introductory video lectures
- Completing beginner-level online courses
- Participating in guided discussions or Q&A sessions
- Taking regular quizzes and practice tests to reinforce learning

Primary Goal:

- Establish a strong knowledge base to support more advanced study.

2. **Intermediate Level**

Time Commitment:

- Schedule: 5 hours/day, 5 days/week
- Duration: 6–8 weeks
- Total Hours: ~150 (including practice exams)
- Outcome: Ready for intermediate-level certification testing

Focus:

- Applying foundational knowledge to real-world scenarios
- Analyzing information and exploring specialized topics within the field

Key Activities:

- Engaging with case studies and scenario-based exercises
- Hands-on lab work or practical assignments
- Participating in group discussions, workshops, or study groups
- Enrolling in intermediate-level courses
- Completing comprehensive practice exams to assess readiness

Primary Goal:

- Develop critical thinking, analytical, and problem-solving skills relevant to the subject area.

3. Advanced Level

Time Commitment:

- Schedule: 8 hours/day, 5 days/week
- Duration: 4–6 weeks
- Total Hours: 160–180 (including practice exams)
- Outcome: Fully prepared for advanced certification testing

Focus:

- Mastering complex concepts and advanced techniques
- Synthesizing knowledge to solve high-level problems and innovate

Key Activities:

- Working on advanced projects or capstone assignments
- Engaging in peer reviews and expert-led seminars
- Intensive lab work or simulations
- Completing advanced-level courses and workshops
- Taking full-length, timed practice exams under exam conditions

Primary Goal:

- Achieve mastery and demonstrate expertise, ready for professional certification or real-world application.

Additional Tips for Success

- Track Progress: Use a learning journal or digital tracker to monitor hours, topics covered, and assessment scores.
- Seek Feedback: Regularly consult with mentors or peers to identify areas for improvement.
- Adjust Pace: Be flexible-adapt the schedule as needed based on comprehension and retention.
- Celebrate Milestones: Recognize achievements at the end of each level to stay motivated.

When planning a structured learning journey, start with the basics—core concepts and terms through reading and beginner courses. Then, move to applying knowledge through case studies, discussions, and hands-on tasks to build problem-solving skills. At the advanced stage, focus on deep study, complex projects, collaboration, and practice exams to master the material. Track progress, get feedback, and celebrate milestones to stay motivated and grow from beginner to advance.

1 AWS Solutions Architect

An AWS Solutions Architect is a professional who designs cloud-based solutions using Amazon Web Services (AWS). They combine technical knowledge with business requirements to create robust, scalable, and secure systems in the cloud.

Key Responsibilities:
Architecting Solutions

Design cloud architectures for web apps, data pipelines, AI systems, IoT setups, etc.

Security & Compliance

Ensure solutions meet security best practices and compliance standards (e.g., HIPAA, GDPR).

Cost Optimization

Choose the right mix of AWS services to balance performance and cost.

Scalability & High Availability

Build systems that can grow automatically based on demand and avoid downtime.

Migration Planning

Help companies move their data and applications from on-premises to AWS cloud.

Core AWS Services They Use:
Compute: EC2 (virtual servers), Lambda (serverless functions)

Storage: S3 (object storage), EBS (block storage)

Databases: RDS (SQL), DynamoDB (NoSQL)

Networking: VPC, Route 53, CloudFront

Security: IAM, KMS, WAF

DevOps Tools: CloudFormation, CodePipeline, CloudWatch

Relevant Certifications:
AWS Certified Solutions Architect – Associate

AWS Certified Solutions Architect – Professional

Salary: $136,000 to $177,000 Annually

Timeline of Certification: 45 to 65 hours-three to four hours per day or 8 to 12 weeks

2 Cloud Engineer

A cloud engineer is an IT professional who designs, builds, manages, and maintains cloud-based systems and infrastructure. Their main job is to help organizations move to the cloud, operate efficiently within it, and ensure security, scalability, and performance.

Core Responsibilities:
Cloud Architecture Design – Planning and designing scalable cloud infrastructure.

Deployment & Automation – Automating services and deployments using Infrastructure-as-Code tools (e.g., Terraform, Ansible).

Maintenance & Monitoring – Ensuring uptime, performance, and reliability of cloud systems.

Security & Compliance – Securing cloud environments with encryption, IAM policies, and compliance frameworks.

Migration – Moving applications, databases, and servers from on-premises to the cloud.

Popular Cloud Platforms They Work With:
Amazon Web Services (AWS)

Microsoft Azure

Google Cloud Platform (GCP)

Sometimes hybrid solutions like IBM Cloud, Oracle Cloud, etc.

Tools and Skills:
DevOps tools (Docker, Kubernetes, Jenkins)

Scripting (Python, Bash, PowerShell)

Networking (VPC, firewalls, load balancers)

CI/CD Pipelines

Monitoring tools (CloudWatch, Datadog, Prometheus)

Educational Background:
Computer Science, Information Technology, or related fields.

   TONY DRAKE

Certifications help: AWS Certified Solutions Architect, Google Cloud Professional Cloud Engineer, Microsoft Certified: Azure Solutions Architect, etc.

Research Angle:
As a researcher, you might explore:

Cloud engineering trends and skills evolution.

Cloud computing's role in research data storage and analysis.

Energy consumption and environmental impact of cloud infrastructure.

The intersection of AI, cloud engineering, and big data.

Salary: $136,000 to $177,000 Annually

Timeline of Certification: 60 to 75 hours of study time-three to four hours per day or five weeks consecutively

3 AWS Solutions Architect

An AWS Solutions Architect is a professional who designs cloud-based solutions using Amazon Web Services (AWS). Their main job is to understand the technical requirements of a project and design scalable, secure, and cost-effective cloud architectures using AWS tools and services.

Here's a breakdown of what an AWS Solutions Architect typically does:

Key Responsibilities:

Design cloud solutions: Build systems that are scalable, reliable, and secure on AWS.

Choose the right services: Select AWS tools that best meet the technical and business needs (e.g., EC2, S3, Lambda, RDS).

Plan for security: Ensure data and systems are protected using best practices like encryption, IAM (Identity and Access Management), and VPCs.

Optimize performance and cost: Make sure the solution is fast and doesn't waste resources.

Collaborate with teams: Work with developers, business stakeholders, and IT staff to implement the architecture.

Troubleshoot and improve existing systems.

Skills Required:
Deep knowledge of AWS services

Understanding of networking, security, and databases

Ability to translate business requirements into technical solutions

Experience with cloud migration and hybrid environments

Familiarity with DevOps and automation tools (like CloudFormation, Terraform, or Ansible)

Certifications (Optional but Valuable):
AWS Certified Solutions Architect – Associate

AWS Certified Solutions Architect – Professional

These certifications validate that someone has the knowledge and experience to design distributed systems on AWS.

Use Case Example:
If a company wants to move its web application from on-premise servers to the cloud, the AWS Solutions Architect would:

Analyze the current setup

Choose the right AWS services (like EC2, RDS, S3)

Design a secure and scalable architecture

Guide the development and migration process

Salary: $136,000 to $250,000 Annually

Timeline of Certification: 60 to 75 hours-three to four hours per day or five weeks consecutively

4 AWS DevOps Engineer

Who is an AWS DevOps Engineer?
An AWS DevOps Engineer is someone who uses Amazon Web Services (AWS) tools to help developers build, test, and release software faster and more efficiently.

What does DevOps mean?
DevOps = Development + Operations

It's a way of working where software developers and IT operations teams collaborate.

The goal is to build better software, fix problems quickly, and automate tasks (like testing, deployment, etc.).

What does an AWS DevOps Engineer do?
Automates software development tasks

For example, when a developer uploads code, the engineer sets up systems to automatically test and deploy it.

Uses AWS tools like:

EC2 – virtual servers

S3 – cloud storage

CodePipeline – automates code changes

CloudFormation – sets up AWS resources with code

CloudWatch – monitors systems

Ensures apps run smoothly

Keeps apps online, fast, and secure.

Quickly fixes issues when something breaks.

Skills an AWS DevOps Engineer needs:
Knowledge of AWS services

Coding skills (like Python, Bash, or JavaScript)

Understanding of CI/CD pipelines (Continuous Integration/Continuous Deployment)

Experience with Linux or Windows servers

Familiarity with Git, Docker, Kubernetes (optional but helpful)

Why is this role important?
Companies want to move faster and be more efficient.

AWS DevOps Engineers help them by automating and optimizing how software is built and delivered.

Salary: $87,000 to $174,000 Annually

Timeline of Certification: 60 to 75 hours of required study time-three to four hours per day or five weeks consecutively

5 AWS SysOps Administrator

Who is an AWS DevOps Administrator?
An AWS DevOps Administrator is a person who manages the tools and processes that help developers and IT teams work together to build, test, and release software faster and more reliably — specifically using Amazon Web Services (AWS).
Let's break it down:

AWS (Amazon Web Services)
This is a cloud platform that offers storage, computing power, databases, and many other services. It's like a big toolbox companies use to run websites, apps, and software on the internet.

DevOps

DevOps stands for Development + Operations.

It's a way of working where developers and system administrators (Ops) collaborate closely. The goal is to:

- Develop software quickly
- Test it effectively
- Deploy it reliably
- Continuously improve the process

Administrator

An administrator is someone who sets up, manages, and monitors these systems and tools to make sure everything runs smoothly.

What does an AWS DevOps Administrator do?

1. Set Up Infrastructure:

   Create and manage servers, databases, and other resources using AWS services like EC2, S3, RDS, etc.

2. Automate Processes:

   Use tools like AWS CodePipeline, CodeDeploy, or Jenkins to automate testing and deployment.

3. Monitor Systems:

   Keep an eye on systems using tools like CloudWatch to ensure everything works correctly.

4. Manage Security:

   Control who can access what (using IAM) and protect systems from threats.

5. Support Teams:

   Help developers and other teams with tools, access, and automation to make their work easier and faster.

Skills Needed

- Knowledge of Linux and scripting (like Bash or Python)
- Familiarity with cloud computing and networking

- Understanding of CI/CD (Continuous Integration/Continuous Deployment)
- Use of version control systems like Git
- Experience with AWS services

Why is it important?
An AWS DevOps Admin helps companies:
- Save time
- Reduce errors
- Improve software quality
- Scale systems easily

Salary: $124,000 to $164,000 Annually

Timeline of Certification: 80 to 95 hours of required study time-three to four hours per day or five weeks consecutively

6 AWS Data Engineer

Who is an AWS Data Engineer?
An AWS Data Engineer is a professional who works with Amazon Web Services (AWS) to manage and process large amounts of data. Their main job is to collect, store, clean, and move data so that businesses can use it for analysis and decision-making.

What Does an AWS Data Engineer Do?
Here are some common tasks:

Collecting Data

They gather data from different sources like websites, databases, apps, or sensors.

Storing Data

They store the data using AWS services like:

Amazon S3 (for files)

Amazon RDS or Amazon Redshift (for databases)

AWS Glue (for data catalogs and ETL)

Processing Data

They clean and transform the data so it can be used in reports or dashboards.

They use tools like AWS Glue, Amazon EMR, or Apache Spark.

Moving Data

They build pipelines to move data automatically from one place to another.

They use services like AWS Data Pipeline or Amazon Kinesis.

Making Data Available

They make sure the data is ready for data analysts, data scientists, or business teams to use.

Skills Needed

Knowledge of AWS services

Programming (Python, SQL, or Scala)

Understanding of ETL (Extract, Transform, Load)

Data modeling and database management

Big data tools like Spark or Hadoop

Salary: $114,000 to $177,000 Annually

Timeline of Certification: 70 to 80 hours of required study time-four to five hours per day or four weeks consecutively

7 AWS Machine Learning Engineer Associate

What is an AWS Machine Learning Engineer Associate?

An AWS Machine Learning Engineer is someone who builds and manages machine learning (ML) models using tools and services provided by Amazon Web Services (AWS).

Let's break it down:
AWS (Amazon Web Services) is a cloud platform that offers many services for computing, storage, databases, and more, including tools specifically for machine learning.

Machine Learning (ML) is a field of artificial intelligence (AI) where computers learn from data and make predictions or decisions without being directly programmed for every task.

Engineer means a person who designs and builds systems.

So, what does an AWS ML Engineer do?

Here are some of their main tasks:

Collect and prepare data – They gather data from different sources and clean it up so it can be used for training ML models.

Build ML models – They use AWS tools like Amazon SageMaker to train models that can recognize patterns or make decisions.

Evaluate and improve models – They test how well the models work and make changes to improve accuracy.

Deploy models to production – They make the models available for use in real-world applications (e.g., recommending products, detecting fraud, etc.).

Monitor and maintain models – After deployment, they keep an eye on the models to make sure they continue working well.

Tools they often use:
Amazon SageMaker

AWS Lambda

Amazon S3 (Storage)

AWS Glue (Data preparation)

Amazon CloudWatch (Monitoring)

Why is this role important?
Machine learning is used in many areas—healthcare, finance, e-commerce, entertainment—and AWS is one of the most popular platforms to run these ML applications. So AWS Machine Learning Engineers play a key role in turning data into smart solutions.

Salary: $100,000 to $190,000 Annually

Timeline of Certification: 70 to 80 hours of required study time-four to five hours per day or four weeks consecutively

8 AWS Lambda Developer (Serverless)

What is an AWS Lambda Developer?
An AWS Lambda Developer is someone who builds and manages small programs that run in the cloud using a service called AWS Lambda.

Let's break that down:

☁ What is AWS Lambda?
AWS Lambda is a tool from Amazon Web Services (AWS) that lets you run code without needing to manage servers. It's called serverless computing.

Imagine you have a program, and instead of running it on your laptop or a big server, you just give it to AWS, and AWS runs it only when needed. You don't have to worry about starting or stopping it—it just works in response to events.

What does an AWS Lambda Developer do?
A Lambda Developer:

Writes code (usually in Python, JavaScript, or other languages)

Uploads it to AWS Lambda

Sets up triggers (like "run this code when someone uploads a file" or "run this every 5 minutes")

Connects it with other AWS services (like databases, storage, etc.)

Example Use Cases
Resize a photo automatically after someone uploads it.

Send a welcome email when a user signs up.

Handle payment events in an online store.

Skills Needed
Programming (Python, Node.js, Java, etc.)

Understanding of cloud basics (especially AWS)

Familiarity with APIs and event-driven systems

Problem-solving mindset!

Why It's Cool for Students
You can start small and build cool projects.

No need to buy servers.

You only pay for what you use.

It's in demand—many companies love serverless!

Salary: $110,000 to $190,000 Annually

Timeline of Certification: 25 to 40 hours of required study time-four to five hours per day or four weeks consecutively

9 AWS Cloud Consultant

What is an AWS Cloud Consultant?

An AWS Cloud Consultant is someone who helps businesses use Amazon Web Services (AWS) to store data, run applications, and manage their IT resources in the cloud.

Let's break that down:

What is the Cloud?
The cloud means using the internet to access servers, storage, and applications instead of using physical computers or hard drives.

What is AWS?
Amazon Web Services (AWS) is a popular cloud platform offered by Amazon. It provides over 200 services like:

Storing files (like Google Drive)

Running websites or apps

Managing databases

Securing data

What Does an AWS Cloud Consultant Do?
An AWS Cloud Consultant:

Helps companies plan how to move to the cloud

Sets up and configures AWS services

Makes sure everything is safe and cost-effective

Troubleshoots any issues

Trains employees on how to use AWS tools

Example:
A company wants to store its customer data online. The AWS Cloud Consultant:

Suggests the best AWS tools (like Amazon S3 for storage)

Sets them up properly

Makes sure the data is protected

Teaches the staff how to use it

Salary: $122,000 to $141,000 Annually

Timeline of Certification: 25 to 40 hours of required study time-four to five hours per day or four weeks consecutively

10 AWS Network Engineer

What is an AWS Network Engineer?
An AWS Network Engineer is someone who designs, builds, manages, and troubleshoots computer networks using Amazon Web Services (AWS) – which is a popular cloud computing platform.

Think of it like this:

- Imagine a school has many computers that need to connect to each other and the internet.
- Now imagine doing that same thing, but in the cloud, for big companies.

- That's what AWS Network Engineers do — but using AWS tools instead of physical wires and routers.

What Does an AWS Network Engineer Do?

Some of their main tasks include:

- Setting up networks in the cloud (like Virtual Private Clouds or VPCs)
- Making sure data can travel safely and quickly between different parts of a system
- Protecting networks with firewalls and security settings
- Connecting on-premise data centers (real buildings) to cloud networks
- Troubleshooting network issues when things go wrong

Skills Needed:

To become an AWS Network Engineer, you usually need to learn:

- Networking basics (IP addresses, DNS, firewalls, etc.)
- Cloud computing, especially how AWS works
- Security practices
- Tools like:
  - AWS VPC
  - AWS Direct Connect
  - Route 53
  - Network Load Balancer (NLB)

How to Get Started as a Student:

1. Learn basic computer networking
2. Study AWS (start with the AWS Certified Cloud Practitioner course)
3. Try the AWS Certified Advanced Networking – Specialty (for more advanced knowledge)
4. Practice with AWS Free Tier (you can test AWS tools for free)
5. Build simple cloud projects

Salary: $89,000 to $143,000 Annually

Timeline of Certification: 25 to 40 hours of required study time-four to five hours per day or four weeks consecutively

11 AWS Database Administrator

An AWS Database Administrator is someone who manages and maintains databases on Amazon Web Services (AWS) — which is a popular cloud computing platform used by many companies around the world.

What They Do:

1. Set Up Databases: Create and configure databases using AWS tools like Amazon RDS, DynamoDB, or Aurora.
2. Monitor Performance: Make sure the databases run smoothly and efficiently.
3. Backup and Restore: Regularly back up data and be ready to restore it if something goes wrong.
4. Security: Protect databases from unauthorized access or attacks.
5. Troubleshooting: Fix problems when databases don't work as expected.
6. Optimize: Tune and improve the speed and performance of databases.

Tools They Use:

- Amazon RDS (Relational Database Service)
- Amazon Aurora
- Amazon DynamoDB
- Amazon Redshift (for data warehouses)

Skills Needed:
- Knowledge of SQL and database management
- Understanding of cloud computing
- Familiarity with AWS services
- Problem-solving and attention to detail

Salary: $80,000 to $141,000 Annually

Timeline of Certification: 25 to 40 hours of required study time-four to five hours per day or four weeks consecutively

12 AWS Big Data Specialist

An AWS Big Data Specialist is someone who has advanced skills in using Amazon Web Services (AWS) to manage, process, and analyze big data—which means large and complex data sets that are too big for traditional data-processing tools.

Here's a simple breakdown:

What they do:

- Work with huge amounts of data from websites, apps, sensors, etc.
- Use AWS tools to store, move, and analyze data.
- Help businesses make smart decisions using data insights.

Common AWS tools they use:

- Amazon S3 – for storing data.
- Amazon EMR – for processing big data using Hadoop or Spark.
- Amazon Redshift – a fast data warehouse.

- AWS Glue – to move and transform data.
- Amazon Kinesis – for real-time data streaming.

Why it matters:

Almost every industry now uses data to understand customers, improve products, and run operations better. An AWS Big Data Specialist helps companies handle all that data securely, quickly, and cost-effectively in the cloud.

How to become one:

- Learn the basics of cloud computing and AWS.
- Study big data concepts like data lakes, ETL, and analytics.
- Get hands-on experience with AWS tools.
- Consider getting the AWS Certified Data Analytics – Specialty certification.

Salary: $80,000 to $141,000 Annually
Timeline of Certification: 25 to 40 hours of required study time-four to five hours per day or four weeks consecutively

13 AWS Migration Specialist

An AWS Migration Specialist is someone who helps move applications, data, and IT systems from a company's current environment (like their own servers or another cloud platform) to Amazon Web Services (AWS)—which is a popular cloud computing platform.

Here's what they typically do:

1. Assess the Current Environment
    They look at what the company already has (servers, apps, data-bases, etc.) and figure out what needs to be moved to AWS.

2. Plan the Migration
    They create a step-by-step plan on how to move everything safely and efficiently without breaking anything.

3. Migrate the Systems
    They carry out the actual migration—moving data, apps, and workloads to AWS.

4. Test and Optimize
    After the migration, they test everything to make sure it works well and look for ways to make it run even better on AWS.

5. Train and Support
    They might also help the company's staff understand how to use AWS or deal with any post-migration issues.

Skills Needed:

- Knowledge of AWS services (like EC2, S3, RDS)
- Experience with cloud computing and networking
- Problem-solving and planning skills
- Tools like AWS Migration Hub, AWS Database Migration Service, or third-party tools

If you're a student interested in becoming one, you can start by:

- Learning cloud basics (AWS offers free courses)
- Getting certified (e.g., AWS Certified Solutions Architect – Associate)
- Practicing on AWS Free Tier

Salary: $80,000 to $141,000 Annually

Timeline of Certification: 25 to 40 hours of required study time-four to five hours per day or four weeks consecutively

14 AWS Technical Trainer

An AWS Technical Trainer is someone who teaches people how to use Amazon Web Services (AWS) — a popular cloud computing platform used by businesses and developers all over the world.

Here's what an AWS Technical Trainer typically does:

What They Do:

1. Teach Cloud Concepts
    They explain how AWS services like storage, servers, databases, and networking work.
2. Conduct Training Sessions
    They lead classes (online or in-person) to help students, professionals, or companies learn AWS.
3. Prepare Learning Materials
    They create presentations, labs, and guides that help others understand AWS tools and services.
4. Help People Get Certified
    They train students to pass AWS certification exams (like AWS Cloud Practitioner, AWS Solutions Architect, etc.).
5. Stay Updated
    They constantly learn about new AWS tools and updates to keep their teaching current.

Skills Needed:

- Strong knowledge of cloud computing and AWS.
- Good communication and teaching skills.
- Certifications like AWS Certified Solutions Architect or AWS Certified Developer.
- Experience with programming (like Python, JavaScript, etc.) is helpful but not always required.

Salary: $65,000 to $103,000 Annually

Timeline of Certification: 25 to 40 hours of required study time-four to five hours per day or four weeks consecutively

15 AWS Support Engineer

AWS Support Engineer is a technical expert who helps customers solve problems related to Amazon Web Services (AWS) — a cloud platform used by businesses to run websites, apps, databases, and more.

What They Do:

- Help customers: When companies have issues with AWS (like servers not working or services being slow), the support engineer helps fix them.
- Troubleshoot problems: They investigate what went wrong and find solutions.
- Guide customers: They explain how to use AWS services correctly and safely.
- Work with engineers: Sometimes, they work with other AWS teams to fix complex issues.

Skills They Need:

- Knowledge of cloud computing and AWS services.
- Understanding of Linux/Windows systems.
- Programming or scripting skills (like Python, Bash, or PowerShell).
- Good communication skills to explain technical things clearly.

Example:

If a company's website goes down and it's hosted on AWS, a support engineer helps them figure out what happened and get it running again.

Salary: $61,000 to $120,000 Annually

Timeline of Certification: 25 to 40 hours of required study time-four to five hours per day or four weeks consecutively

16 AWS Infrastructure Engineer

An AWS Infrastructure Engineer is someone who builds and manages computer systems using Amazon Web Services (AWS) — which is one of the biggest cloud platforms in the world.

What does that mean?

Instead of using physical computers or servers in an office, companies today often use cloud platforms like AWS to:

- Store data
- Run websites and apps

- Process information
- Keep everything secure and available all the time

An AWS Infrastructure Engineer makes sure all of this works smoothly. They:

- Set up and manage cloud servers (called EC2 instances)
- Store and organize data (using tools like S3 and databases)
- Make sure websites and apps don't go down
- Improve speed and security
- Create automated systems that reduce manual work

In short:

An AWS Infrastructure Engineer is like a digital architect who builds and maintains the tech "backbone" of a company in the cloud.

If you're a student and interested in this career, you might want to learn:

- Cloud computing basics (especially AWS)
- Networking and security
- Linux and Windows systems
- Automation tools like Terraform or Ansible
- Programming (Python or Bash)

Salary: $127,000 to $175,000 Annually

Timeline of Certification: 25 to 40 hours of required study time-four to five hours per day or four weeks consecutively

17 AWS Cloud Cost Optimization Analyst

An AWS Cloud Cost Optimization Analyst is someone who helps organizations save money and spend wisely when using Amazon Web Services (AWS) — a popular cloud computing platform.

Here's what they do in simple terms:

1. Analyze Cloud Usage

They look at how a company is using AWS services like servers, storage, databases, etc.

2. Identify Wasted Spending

They check for things like:

- Unused or underused services (e.g., servers running when no one is using them)
- Overprovisioned resources (e.g., too much power or memory than needed)
- Expensive services that can be replaced by cheaper ones

3. Recommend Cost-Saving Strategies

They suggest ways to reduce costs, such as:

- Turning off services at night or weekends
- Choosing better pricing models (e.g., Reserved Instances, Spot Instances)
- Cleaning up unused data storage

4. Work with Teams

They work with engineers, finance teams, and IT departments to make sure changes are implemented.

Skills They Often Have:

- Basic knowledge of AWS services (like EC2, S3, Lambda)
- Understanding of billing and pricing models

- Ability to use AWS tools like AWS Cost Explorer, Budgets, or Trusted Advisor
- Analytical thinking and Excel skills
- Sometimes scripting or automation (e.g., Python, AWS CLI)

Why Is It Important?

Because cloud bills can get very high if not managed properly. This role helps companies:

- Avoid surprise bills
- Save thousands (or even millions) of dollars
- Use the cloud more efficiently

Salary: $101,000 to $168,000 Annually

Timeline of Certification: 25 to 40 hours of required study time-four to five hours per day or four weeks consecutively

18 AWS IoT Developer

What is an AWS IoT Developer?

An AWS IoT Developer is someone who builds applications and systems using Amazon Web Services (AWS) to connect and manage Internet of Things (IoT) devices.

Let's break that down:

- IoT (Internet of Things):
  This refers to physical devices like sensors, smart appliances, wearables, or machines that connect to the internet and collect or send data.

- AWS (Amazon Web Services):
  AWS is a cloud platform that provides tools and services to help developers store data, run applications, and manage devices online.

What Does an AWS IoT Developer Do?

Here are some of the things they do:

1. Connect devices to the cloud using AWS IoT Core.
2. Send and receive data between devices and the cloud.
3. Store and analyze data from devices using AWS tools like DynamoDB, S3, or AWS Lambda.
4. Monitor devices and set up rules to take action when something important happens.
5. Secure communication between devices and AWS services.

Why is this important?

IoT is used in smart homes, factories, agriculture, healthcare, and more. AWS gives developers the tools to build smart systems that can improve efficiency, safety, and convenience.

Example:

Imagine you're building a smart farm system. You could use AWS IoT to:

- Connect sensors in the soil to check moisture levels.
- Send the data to AWS.
- Automatically turn on watering when the soil is dry.
- Notify the farmer via a mobile app.

Salary: $107,000 to $160,000 Annually

Timeline of Certification: 25 to 40 hours of required study time-four to five hours per day or four weeks consecutively

19 AWS CI/CD Pipeline Engineer

What is CI/CD?

CI/CD stands for:

- CI (Continuous Integration): Developers regularly upload (or "commit") their code to a shared system. This code is automatically built and tested to make sure it works properly.
- CD (Continuous Delivery or Deployment): After the code passes tests, it's automatically deployed to a server (for example, a website or app).

This helps software teams deliver updates faster and with fewer bugs.

What does an AWS CI/CD Pipeline Engineer do?

They use AWS tools like:

- CodeCommit – like GitHub, for storing code.
- CodeBuild – to compile and test code.
- CodeDeploy – to push updates to servers or cloud environments.
- CodePipeline – to automate all the steps (build, test, deploy).
- CloudFormation or Terraform – to automate infrastructure setup.
- EC2, Lambda, S3, ECS, etc. – to host apps or services.

Their job is to:

1. Create pipelines that automate software delivery.
2. Ensure code is tested and safe before it goes live.
3. Fix problems fast if something breaks in the pipeline.
4. Collaborate with developers and help them release updates more efficiently.

Example:

Let's say your team builds a mobile app. When a developer uploads new code:

1. AWS automatically builds the new version.
2. It runs tests to make sure the app still works.
3. If everything looks good, AWS deploys the new version to your server or app store.

Skills Needed:

- AWS (especially DevOps services)
- Git (code version control)
- Linux basics
- Docker/Kubernetes (sometimes)
- Scripting (like Python or Bash)
- Understanding of CI/CD principles

Salary: $80,000 to $120,000 Annually

Timeline of Certification: 25 to 40 hours of required study time-four to five hours per day or four weeks consecutively

20 AWS Compliance & Governance Specialist

An AWS Compliance & Governance Specialist is someone who helps organizations make sure they are following the rules and laws when using Amazon Web Services (AWS) — which is a cloud computing platform.

What does this person do?

They focus on:

1. Compliance
    Making sure the company is following all the legal, industry, and security rules (like GDPR, HIPAA, etc.).
2. Governance
    Creating policies, procedures, and controls to manage how AWS services are used safely and responsibly.
3. Audits and Reports
    Helping with security audits, checking for risks, and generating compliance reports.
4. Training
    Teaching staff about best practices and policies for staying secure and compliant on AWS.
5. Monitoring
    Using tools to track activity, catch issues early, and ensure the company's data is protected.

Example:

If a hospital stores patient records on AWS, the Compliance & Governance Specialist makes sure the data is stored in a way that follows health privacy laws.

Salary: $55,000 to $229,000 Annually

Timeline of Certification: 25 to 40 hours of required study time-four to five hours per day or four weeks consecutively

21 Cloud Architecture

As a student, understanding the role of a Cloud Architect can be a great career inspiration, especially if you're interested in cloud computing, IT infrastructure, and designing scalable systems. Here's a simple breakdown:

Who is a Cloud Architect?

A Cloud Architect is an IT professional who designs, plans, and oversees the implementation of cloud computing solutions for businesses. They ensure that cloud systems (like AWS, Azure, or Google Cloud) are secure, scalable, and cost-effective.

Key Responsibilities:

1. Design Cloud Solutions – Create blueprints for cloud infrastructure (servers, storage, networking).
2. Migrate to Cloud – Help companies move from on-premise systems to the cloud.
3. Optimize Costs & Performance – Ensure the cloud setup is efficient and cost-effective.
4. Security & Compliance – Implement security measures to protect data.
5. Automation & DevOps – Use tools like Kubernetes, Docker, and CI/CD pipelines.

Skills Required:

- Knowledge of cloud platforms (AWS, Azure, GCP).
- Understanding of networking, security, and databases.
- Familiarity with Infrastructure as Code (IaC) (Terraform, CloudFormation).

- Coding/scripting (Python, Bash, PowerShell).
- Problem-solving & communication skills.

How to Start as a Student?

1. Learn Cloud Basics – Take free courses on AWS/Azure/GCP (e.g., AWS Educate, Microsoft Learn).
2. Get Certified – Start with AWS Certified Cloud Practitioner or Azure Fundamentals.
3. Hands-on Practice – Use free-tier cloud accounts to deploy projects.
4. Explore DevOps – Learn Docker, Kubernetes, and CI/CD tools.
5. Join Cloud Communities – Engage in forums, hackathons, and open-source projects.

Career Path:

- Entry-Level: Cloud Support Engineer → Cloud Administrator
- Mid-Level: Cloud Engineer → DevOps Engineer
- Senior-Level: Cloud Architect → Cloud Consultant

Salary Expectations (Varies by Region & Experience):

- Entry-Level: 70K–70K–100K/year
- Experienced: 120K–120K–180K/year

Timeline of Certification: 25 to 40 hours of required study time-four to five hours per day or four weeks consecutively

22 DevOps Engineer

As a student, you might be curious about DevOps Engineering, which is one of the most in-demand and exciting roles in the tech industry today. Let me break it down for you in simple terms.

What is a DevOps Engineer?

A DevOps Engineer is an IT professional who bridges the gap between software development (Dev) and IT operations (Ops). They focus on automating and streamlining the software delivery process to make it faster, more reliable, and more efficient.

Key Responsibilities of a DevOps Engineer:

1. Automation – Writing scripts (Python, Bash) and using tools (like Ansible, Terraform) to automate repetitive tasks.
2. Continuous Integration & Continuous Deployment (CI/CD) – Setting up pipelines (using Jenkins, GitHub Actions, GitLab CI) to automatically build, test, and deploy code.
3. Cloud Computing – Managing cloud infrastructure (AWS, Azure, GCP) to host applications.
4. Monitoring & Logging – Using tools like Prometheus, Grafana, and ELK Stack to monitor system health.
5. Containerization & Orchestration – Working with Docker and Kubernetes to deploy scalable applications.
6. Collaboration – Working closely with developers, testers, and sysadmins to improve workflows.

Why Learn DevOps?

High Demand – Companies need DevOps skills to deliver software faster.
Great Salaries – DevOps Engineers are among the highest-paid in IT.

Future-Proof Career – Cloud and automation are growing rapidly.

How to Become a DevOps Engineer (Roadmap for Students)

1. Learn Linux & Scripting (Bash, Python)
2. Understand Version Control (Git, GitHub/GitLab)
3. Learn CI/CD Tools (Jenkins, GitHub Actions)
4. Master Cloud Platforms (AWS/Azure/GCP)
5. Learn Infrastructure as Code (IaC) (Terraform, Ansible)
6. Explore Containers & Kubernetes (Docker, Kubernetes)
7. Practice Monitoring & Logging (Prometheus, Grafana)

Final Advice

- Start with small projects (e.g., automate a task with Python).
- Get hands-on with free cloud tiers (AWS Free Tier, Google Cloud).
- Contribute to open-source DevOps projects.
- Consider certifications like AWS Certified DevOps Engineer or Certified Kubernetes Administrator (CKA).
- Entry-Level: 70K–70K–117K/year
- Experienced: 137K–145K–160K/year

Timeline of Certification: 25 to 40 hours of required study time-four to five hours per day or four weeks consecutively

23 Site Reliability Engineer

A Site Reliability Engineer (SRE) is a role in the tech industry that combines software engineering and IT operations to build and maintain highly scalable, reliable, and efficient software systems.

What Does an SRE Do?

SREs ensure that websites, apps, and services run smoothly with minimal downtime. Their key responsibilities include:

1. Monitoring Systems – Using tools to track performance and detect issues.
2. Automating Tasks – Writing scripts to reduce manual work (e.g., auto-fixing problems).
3. Incident Response – Troubleshooting outages and improving system resilience.
4. Performance Optimization – Making systems faster and more efficient.
5. Capacity Planning – Ensuring systems can handle growth in users or data.
6. Collaborating with Dev Teams – Helping developers build more reliable software.

Skills Needed to Become an SRE

- Programming (Python, Go, Bash, etc.)
- Cloud & DevOps (AWS/GCP/Azure, Kubernetes, Docker)
- Monitoring Tools (Prometheus, Grafana, ELK Stack)
- Linux/Networking Basics
- Problem-Solving & Automation Mindset

Why Should Students Consider SRE?

- High demand & good salaries 💰
- Mix of coding and infrastructure work
- Critical role in big tech companies (Google, Netflix, etc.)

How to Start as a Student?

1. Learn Linux, scripting, and cloud basics.
2. Work on projects involving automation (e.g., deploy a website with CI/CD).
3. Contribute to open-source or intern in DevOps/SRE roles.

Salary: $88,000 to $103,000 Annually

Timeline of Certification: 25 to 40 hours of required study time-four to five hours per day or four weeks consecutively

24 Kubernetes Engineer

As a student, you might be curious about what a Kubernetes Engineer does and how you can become one. Let me break it down for you in simple terms.

What is a Kubernetes Engineer?

A Kubernetes Engineer is a DevOps or Cloud Engineer who specializes in Kubernetes (K8s), an open-source platform for automating the deployment, scaling, and management of containerized applications (like Docker containers).

Key Responsibilities of a Kubernetes Engineer:

1. Deploying & Managing Kubernetes Clusters – Setting up and maintaining Kubernetes environments (on cloud providers like AWS, GCP, or Azure, or on-premises).

2. Automating Deployments – Using tools like Helm, ArgoCD, or Flux to deploy applications efficiently.
3. Scaling Applications – Ensuring apps can handle traffic spikes by configuring auto-scaling.
4. Monitoring & Troubleshooting – Using tools like Prometheus, Grafana, and logging systems (ELK stack) to keep applications running smoothly.
5. Security & Compliance – Managing access control (RBAC), network policies, and securing containerized workloads.
6. CI/CD Pipelines – Integrating Kubernetes with CI/CD tools like Jenkins, GitHub Actions, or GitLab CI.

Skills Needed to Become a Kubernetes Engineer:

- Containers & Docker (Kubernetes runs containers, so Docker knowledge is essential).
- Kubernetes Fundamentals (Pods, Deployments, Services, Ingress, StatefulSets, etc.).
- Cloud Platforms (AWS EKS, Google GKE, Azure AKS).
- Infrastructure as Code (IaC) (Terraform, Ansible).
- Scripting & Automation (Bash, Python, Go).
- Networking & Security (CNI plugins, Calico, Istio for service mesh).

How to Start as a Student?

1. Learn Linux & Containers (Docker) – Start with the basics.
2. Take a Kubernetes Course (e.g., "Kubernetes for Beginners" on Udemy, or official Kubernetes documentation).
3. Get Hands-on Experience – Use Minikube or Kind to run Kubernetes locally.
4. Earn Certifications (Optional but helpful):

- o   Certified Kubernetes Administrator (CKA) – Best for engineers.
  - o   Certified Kubernetes Application Developer (CKAD) – If you're into app development.
5. Contribute to Open Source – Work on Kubernetes-related projects on GitHub.

Career Path & Salary

- Entry-Level: DevOps / Cloud Engineer (~80K–80K–120K).
- Mid-Level: Kubernetes Engineer (~120K–120K–160K).
- Senior-Level: Kubernetes Architect (~$160K+).

Why Learn Kubernetes?

- High demand in cloud computing & DevOps.
- Used by top companies (Google, Netflix, Spotify).
- Great career growth & salary potential.

25 Terraform Engineer

As a student, you might be curious about what a Terraform Engineer does and how it fits into the tech industry. Let me break it down for you in simple terms.

Who is a Terraform Engineer?

A Terraform Engineer (often called an Infrastructure as Code (IaC) Engineer or DevOps Engineer) is a professional who specializes in using HashiCorp Terraform to automate and manage cloud infrastructure. They write code to define, provision, and manage servers, databases, networks, and other cloud resources instead of manually setting them up.

Key Responsibilities of a Terraform Engineer

1. Writing Terraform Code – Creating configuration files (.tf) to define cloud infrastructure (AWS, Azure, GCP, etc.).
2. Automating Deployments – Using Terraform to spin up servers, Kubernetes clusters, databases, etc., with code.
3. Managing State – Tracking infrastructure changes using Terraform state files.
4. Collaborating with DevOps & Developers – Working in CI/CD pipelines to ensure smooth deployments.
5. Security & Compliance – Implementing best practices for secure infrastructure (e.g., using Terraform modules, remote backends).
6. Troubleshooting – Fixing issues related to infrastructure provisioning.

Skills Needed to Become a Terraform Engineer

- Terraform Basics – Understand terraform init, plan, apply, destroy, modules, providers.
- Cloud Knowledge – AWS, Azure, or Google Cloud (Terraform works with all major clouds).
- Version Control (Git) – Managing Terraform code in repositories.
- CI/CD Tools – Jenkins, GitHub Actions, GitLab CI.
- Scripting (Optional) – Bash, Python, or PowerShell for automation.
- Networking Basics – Understanding VPCs, subnets, security groups.

Why Learn Terraform as a Student?

- High Demand – Many companies use Terraform for cloud automation.
- Career Growth – Terraform skills lead to roles like DevOps Engineer, Cloud Engineer, or SRE.
- Hands-on Learning – You can practice for free using Terraform with cloud free tiers (AWS Free Tier, Azure Free Account).

- Certifications – HashiCorp offers a Terraform Associate certification, which is great for your resume.

How to Get Started?

1. Learn Basics – Try Terraform's official docs.
2. Practice – Deploy a simple EC2 instance on AWS using Terraform.
3. Build Projects – Automate a full web app infrastructure (server + database + load balancer).
4. Get Certified – Take the HashiCorp Certified: Terraform Associate exam.

Final Thoughts

A Terraform Engineer is a key player in modern cloud infrastructure. If you enjoy automation, coding, and cloud technologies, learning Terraform can open up exciting career opportunities in DevOps and Cloud Engineering.

Salary: $67,000 to $185,000 Annually

Timeline of Certification: 25 to 40 hours of required study time-four to five hours per day or four weeks consecutively

26 CI/CD Pipeline Engineer

A CI/CD Pipeline Engineer is a specialized role in software development and DevOps that focuses on designing, implementing, and maintaining Continuous Integration (CI) and Continuous Deployment/Delivery (CD) pipelines. These pipelines automate the process of building, testing, and deploying software, ensuring faster, more reliable releases.

What Does a CI/CD Pipeline Engineer Do?

1. Designs & Implements CI/CD Pipelines
   ○ Sets up tools like Jenkins, GitLab CI/CD, GitHub Actions, CircleCI, or Azure DevOps to automate code integration and deployment.
   ○ Ensures pipelines are efficient, scalable, and secure.
2. Automates Testing
   ○ Integrates unit tests, integration tests, and end-to-end tests into the pipeline.
   ○ Uses tools like Selenium, JUnit, pytest, or Cypress.
3. Manages Deployment Strategies
   ○ Implements blue-green deployments, canary releases, or rolling updates to minimize downtime.
   ○ Works with containerization (Docker) and orchestration tools (Kubernetes).
4. Ensures Security & Compliance
   ○ Integrates security scans (SAST/DAST) using tools like SonarQube, Snyk, or OWASP ZAP.
   ○ Manages secrets and access controls.
5. Monitors & Optimizes Pipelines
   ○ Tracks pipeline performance (speed, failure rates).
   ○ Fixes bottlenecks and improves reliability.
6. Collaborates with Teams
   ○ Works with developers, QA, and operations (DevOps culture) to streamline workflows.

Skills Needed to Become a CI/CD Pipeline Engineer

✓ Scripting & Coding (Bash, Python, Groovy, YAML)
✓ CI/CD Tools (Jenkins, GitHub Actions, GitLab CI/CD)
✓ Version Control (Git, GitHub, GitLab)
✓ Containerization (Docker, Kubernetes)

- ✓ Cloud Platforms (AWS, Azure, GCP)
- ✓ Infrastructure as Code (IaC) (Terraform, Ansible)
- ✓ Monitoring & Logging (Prometheus, Grafana, ELK Stack)

Why Is This Role Important?

- Faster software releases with fewer errors.
- Better collaboration between development and operations.
- Higher-quality code due to automated testing.

How to Start as a Student?

1. Learn Git & GitHub (try automating workflows with GitHub Actions).
2. Experiment with Docker (containerize a simple app).
3. Set up a Jenkins pipeline for a small project.
4. Explore cloud platforms (AWS/Azure free tiers).
5. Contribute to open-source projects with CI/CD setups.

This role is in high demand as more companies adopt DevOps practices. If you enjoy automation, scripting, and improving software delivery, this could be a great career path

Salary: $100,000 to $180,000 Annually

Timeline of Certification: 25 to 40 hours of required study time-four to five hours per day or four weeks consecutively

27 Cloud Security Engineer

A Cloud Security Engineer is a specialized IT professional responsible for securing cloud-based systems, data, and infrastructure. They design, implement, and maintain security measures to protect cloud environments from cyber threats, unauthorized access, and data breaches.

Key Responsibilities of a Cloud Security Engineer:

1. Cloud Security Architecture – Designing secure cloud infrastructure (AWS, Azure, GCP).
2. Identity & Access Management (IAM) – Managing user permissions and authentication.
3. Data Protection – Encrypting sensitive data and ensuring compliance (GDPR, HIPAA).
4. Threat Detection & Response – Monitoring for security breaches and responding to incidents.
5. Network Security – Configuring firewalls, VPNs, and intrusion detection systems.
6. Compliance & Auditing – Ensuring cloud systems meet industry security standards.
7. Automation & DevSecOps – Integrating security into CI/CD pipelines.

Skills Required:

- ✓ Knowledge of cloud platforms (AWS, Azure, Google Cloud)
- ✓ Understanding of cybersecurity principles (encryption, firewalls, zero trust)
- ✓ Familiarity with compliance frameworks (ISO 27001, SOC 2, NIST)

✓ Scripting (Python, Bash) and automation tools (Terraform, Ansible)

✓ Certifications like CCSP, AWS Security Specialty, CISSP are a plus

Why It's a Great Career Choice:

- High demand (companies are rapidly moving to the cloud).
- Competitive salaries (100K–100K–160K+ depending on experience).
- Continuous learning (evolving threats & technologies).

Since you're a student, you can start by learning cloud platforms (AWS/Azure free tiers), cybersecurity basics, and getting certifications like CompTIA Security+ or AWS Certified Security Specialty.

Salary: $67,000 to $185,000 Annually

Timeline of Certification: 25 to 40 hours of required study time-four to five hours per day or four weeks consecutively

28 Cloud Network Engineer

A Cloud Security Engineer is a specialized IT professional responsible for securing cloud-based systems, data, and infrastructure. They design, implement, and maintain security measures to protect cloud environments from cyber threats, unauthorized access, and data breaches.

Key Responsibilities of a Cloud Security Engineer:

1. Cloud Security Architecture – Designing secure cloud infrastructure (AWS, Azure, GCP).

2. Identity & Access Management (IAM) – Managing user permissions and authentication.
3. Data Protection – Encrypting sensitive data and ensuring compliance (GDPR, HIPAA).
4. Threat Detection & Response – Monitoring for security breaches and responding to incidents.
5. Network Security – Configuring firewalls, VPNs, and intrusion detection systems.
6. Compliance & Auditing – Ensuring cloud systems meet industry security standards.
7. Automation & DevSecOps – Integrating security into CI/CD pipelines.

Skills Required:

- ✓ Knowledge of cloud platforms (AWS, Azure, Google Cloud)
- ✓ Understanding of cybersecurity principles (encryption, firewalls, zero trust)
- ✓ Familiarity with compliance frameworks (ISO 27001, SOC 2, NIST)
- ✓ Scripting (Python, Bash) and automation tools (Terraform, Ansible)
- ✓ Certifications like CCSP, AWS Security Specialty, CISSP are a plus

Why It's a Great Career Choice:

- High demand (companies are rapidly moving to the cloud).
- Competitive salaries (100K–100K–160K+ depending on experience).
- Continuous learning (evolving threats & technologies).

Since you're a student, you can start by learning cloud platforms (AWS/Azure free tiers), cybersecurity basics, and getting certifications like CompTIA Security+ or AWS Certified Security Specialty.

Salary: $123,000 to $205,000 Annually

Timeline of Certification: 25 to 40 hours of required study time-four to five hours per day or four weeks consecutively

29 Cloud Database Administrator

As a student exploring career options, you might be curious about what a Cloud Database Administrator (Cloud DBA) does. Here's a simple breakdown:

Who is a Cloud Database Administrator?

A Cloud DBA is an IT professional who manages, maintains, and optimizes databases that are hosted in the cloud (like AWS, Azure, Google Cloud, or Oracle Cloud). They ensure that databases are secure, performant, and available to users.

Key Responsibilities:

1. Database Setup & Migration
   - Deploying databases in the cloud (e.g., Amazon RDS, Azure SQL, Google Cloud SQL).
   - Moving on-premises databases to the cloud.
2. Performance Tuning
   - Optimizing queries and indexes for faster performance.
   - Monitoring database health (CPU, memory, storage usage).

3. Security & Backup Management
   - Setting up access controls (who can read/write data).
   - Ensuring backups and disaster recovery plans are in place.
4. Automation & Scaling
   - Using cloud tools to auto-scale databases based on demand.
   - Automating routine tasks like updates and patches.
5. Troubleshooting
   - Fixing issues like slow queries, crashes, or connectivity problems.

Skills Needed:

- ✓ Database Knowledge: SQL (MySQL, PostgreSQL, SQL Server) & NoSQL (MongoDB, Cassandra).
- ✓ Cloud Platforms: AWS, Azure, or Google Cloud certifications help.
- ✓ Scripting & Automation: Python, Bash, or PowerShell for managing tasks.
- ✓ Monitoring Tools: CloudWatch (AWS), Azure Monitor, or third-party tools like Datadog.

Why Become a Cloud DBA?

- High Demand: Companies are moving databases to the cloud → more jobs.
- Good Salary: Cloud DBAs earn well (often 90K–90K–130K+ depending on experience).
- Hybrid Role: Mix of database admin + cloud skills → more career flexibility.

How to Start as a Student?

- Learn SQL (free courses on Codecademy, Khan Academy).
- Try free cloud tiers (AWS Free Tier, Google Cloud $300 credit).

- Get certified (AWS Certified Database Specialty, Microsoft Azure DBA).
- Practice with real projects (set up a cloud database, migrate data).

Salary: $80,000 to $141,000 Annually

Timeline of Certification: 25 to 40 hours of required study time-four to five hours per day or four weeks consecutively

30 Cloud Automation Engineer

As a student exploring career options, you might find the role of a Cloud Automation Engineer exciting if you're interested in cloud computing, programming, and automation. Here's a breakdown of what it entails:

Who is a Cloud Automation Engineer?

A Cloud Automation Engineer is an IT professional who designs, builds, and manages automated cloud infrastructure and workflows. They use tools and code to eliminate manual processes, making cloud deployments faster, more reliable, and scalable.

Key Responsibilities

1. Infrastructure as Code (IaC) – Automating cloud infrastructure using tools like:
    - Terraform
    - AWS CloudFormation
    - Azure Resource Manager (ARM)
    - Google Cloud Deployment Manager

2. CI/CD Pipelines – Setting up automated build, test, and deployment workflows using:
    - Jenkins
    - GitHub Actions
    - GitLab CI/CD
    - AWS CodePipeline
3. Configuration Management – Automating server setups with tools like:
    - Ansible
    - Chef
    - Puppet
4. Cloud Platform Expertise – Working with providers like:
    - AWS (Amazon Web Services)
    - Microsoft Azure
    - Google Cloud Platform (GCP)
5. Scripting & Programming – Writing automation scripts in languages like:
    - Python
    - Bash
    - PowerShell
6. Monitoring & Optimization – Ensuring cloud systems run efficiently using:
    - Prometheus
    - Grafana
    - AWS CloudWatch

Skills Needed

- ✓ Cloud Fundamentals (Networking, Security, Virtualization)
- ✓ Coding & Scripting (Python, YAML, JSON)
- ✓ DevOps & Agile Practices

✓ Containerization & Orchestration (Docker, Kubernetes)

✓ Problem-Solving & Troubleshooting

Why Become a Cloud Automation Engineer?

- High Demand: Companies are rapidly adopting cloud automation.
- Great Salary: Pays well due to specialized skills.
- Future-Proof: Cloud computing is growing fast.

How to Start as a Student?

1. Learn Cloud Basics – Take free courses on AWS/Azure/GCP.
2. Practice Automation – Try Terraform/Ansible on small projects.
3. Get Certified – Consider AWS Certified DevOps Engineer or Azure DevOps Expert.
4. Build Projects – Automate deployments using GitHub Actions or Jenkins.
5. Internships & Open Source – Gain real-world experience.

Career Path

- Junior Cloud Engineer → Cloud Automation Engineer → Senior/Lead DevOps Engineer
- Opportunities in startups, tech giants, and cloud consulting firms.

Salary: $80,000 to $165,000 Annually

Timeline of Certification: 25 to 40 hours of required study time-four to five hours per day or four weeks consecutively Salary: $123,000 to $205,000 Annually

31 | Cloud Support Engineer

As a student, it's great that you're exploring career options like Cloud Support Engineer. Let me break it down for you in simple terms:

What is a Cloud Support Engineer?

A Cloud Support Engineer is a technical professional who helps customers or internal teams resolve issues related to cloud computing services (like AWS, Azure, or Google Cloud). They troubleshoot problems, optimize cloud infrastructure, and ensure smooth operations for businesses using cloud platforms.

Key Responsibilities:

1. Troubleshooting – Fixing issues related to cloud services (e.g., server errors, network problems, access permissions).
2. Customer Support – Assisting clients via email, chat, or phone to resolve technical problems.
3. Monitoring & Maintenance – Ensuring cloud systems run efficiently and applying updates.
4. Automation & Scripting – Writing scripts (Python, Bash) to automate repetitive tasks.
5. Security & Compliance – Helping implement security best practices in cloud environments.
6. Collaboration – Working with DevOps, developers, and sysadmins to improve cloud solutions.

Skills Required:

✓ Cloud Platforms – AWS, Azure, or Google Cloud (certifications like AWS Certified Cloud Practitioner help).

- ✓ Networking – Understanding of DNS, VPN, Firewalls, Load Balancers.
- ✓ Linux/Windows – Basic system administration skills.
- ✓ Scripting – Python, Bash, or PowerShell for automation.
- ✓ Problem-Solving – Debugging and analytical skills.
- ✓ Communication – Explaining technical issues clearly to non-tech users.

How to Become One (as a Student)?

1. Learn Cloud Basics – Start with free courses on AWS/Azure/GCP (e.g., AWS Free Tier).
2. Get Certified – Entry-level certs like AWS Certified Cloud Practitioner.
3. Practice Hands-on – Use cloud labs (e.g., Qwiklabs, A Cloud Guru).
4. Develop Scripting Skills – Learn Python/Bash for automation.
5. Internships/Projects – Work on cloud-related projects or internships.
6. Apply for Entry-Level Roles – Look for Cloud Support Associate or Technical Support Engineer roles.

Salary & Career Growth:

- Entry-Level Salary: ~80K–105K–170K (varies by location & company).
- Career Path: Can grow into Cloud Engineer, DevOps Engineer, or Solutions Architect.

32 Cloud Migration Specialist

As a student, it's great that you're exploring career paths in technology! A Cloud Migration Specialist is a professional who helps organizations move their data, applications, and IT infrastructure from on-premises (local servers) or legacy systems to cloud platforms like AWS, Microsoft Azure, or Google Cloud.

What Does a Cloud Migration Specialist Do?

1. Assess Current Systems – Evaluates existing IT infrastructure to determine what can be moved to the cloud.
2. Plan Migration Strategy – Decides whether to use a lift-and-shift (quick move), re-platforming (minor optimizations), or re-factoring (rebuilding for cloud-native).
3. Execute Migration – Moves applications, databases, and workloads to the cloud with minimal downtime.
4. Optimize Costs & Performance – Ensures the cloud setup is efficient, secure, and cost-effective.
5. Troubleshoot & Support – Fixes issues during and after migration.

Skills Needed to Become a Cloud Migration Specialist

- ✓ Cloud Platforms – AWS, Azure, or Google Cloud certifications (e.g., AWS Certified Solutions Architect, Azure Administrator).
- ✓ Networking & Security – Understanding of firewalls, VPNs, and cloud security best practices.
- ✓ Virtualization & Containers – Knowledge of VMware, Docker, or Kubernetes.
- ✓ Scripting & Automation – Basics of Python, PowerShell, or Terraform (Infrastructure as Code).

✓ Database & Storage – Experience with SQL/NoSQL databases and cloud storage solutions.

How to Start as a Student?

- Learn cloud fundamentals (free courses on AWS/Azure/GCP).
- Get hands-on with free-tier cloud accounts.
- Work on small migration projects (e.g., moving a website to the cloud).
- Earn entry-level certs like AWS Cloud Practitioner or Microsoft Azure Fundamentals.

Salary: $70,000 to $165,000 Annually

Timeline of Certification: 25 to 40 hours of required study time-four to five hours per day or four weeks consecutively Salary

33 Cloud Cost Optimization Analyst

A Cloud Cost Optimization Analyst is a professional who specializes in analyzing and reducing cloud computing expenses while ensuring optimal performance and resource utilization. If you're a student exploring career options in cloud computing or FinOps (Financial Operations), this role could be a great fit if you enjoy working with cloud technologies, data analysis, and cost management.

Key Responsibilities:

1. Cost Monitoring & Analysis
   - Track cloud spending across platforms like AWS, Azure, or Google Cloud.

o   Identify inefficiencies, wasted resources (e.g., idle instances, over-provisioned services).

2. Optimization Strategies
    o   Recommend rightsizing (adjusting resources to match workload needs).
    o   Implement reserved instances or savings plans for long-term discounts.
    o   Automate scaling to reduce costs during low-usage periods.

3. Budgeting & Forecasting
    o   Predict future cloud costs based on usage trends.
    o   Set budget alerts to prevent overspending.

4. Collaboration
    o   Work with DevOps, engineering, and finance teams to align cloud costs with business goals.

5. Tooling & Reporting
    o   Use tools like AWS Cost Explorer, Azure Cost Management, or third-party solutions (e.g., CloudHealth, Kubecost).
    o   Generate reports for stakeholders showing cost savings and ROI.

Skills Needed:

- Cloud Knowledge: Understanding of AWS/Azure/GCP services.
- Data Analysis: Proficiency in Excel, SQL, or visualization tools (Power BI, Tableau).
- FinOps Principles: Balancing cost, performance, and business needs.
- Automation & Scripting: Familiarity with tools like Terraform, Python, or cloud-native cost automation.

How to Start as a Student:

1. Learn Cloud Basics: Get certified in AWS/Azure fundamentals (e.g., AWS Cloud Practitioner).

2. Practice Cost Monitoring: Use free-tier cloud accounts to analyze spending.

3. Study FinOps: Explore the FinOps Foundation framework.

4. Internships: Look for roles in cloud operations, finance, or IT analytics.

Salary: $70,000 to $165,000 Annually

Timeline of Certification: 25 to 40 hours of required study time-four to five hours per day or four weeks consecutively Salary

34. Cloud Infrastructure Engineer

A Cloud Infrastructure Engineer is an IT professional responsible for designing, deploying, and managing cloud-based systems and services. They work with cloud platforms like AWS, Azure, or Google Cloud to ensure that a company's applications and data run smoothly, securely, and efficiently in the cloud.

What Does a Cloud Infrastructure Engineer Do?

1. Design & Deploy Cloud Systems
    - Set up cloud environments (servers, storage, networking).
    - Automate deployments using Infrastructure as Code (IaC) tools like Terraform, CloudFormation, or Ansible.
2. Manage & Optimize Cloud Resources
    - Monitor performance, scalability, and cost efficiency.
    - Troubleshoot issues and ensure high availability.
3. Security & Compliance
    - Implement security best practices (firewalls, encryption, IAM policies).
    - Ensure compliance with industry standards (GDPR, HIPAA, etc.).

4. Automation & DevOps
   - Work with CI/CD pipelines (Jenkins, GitHub Actions, GitLab CI).
   - Use containerization (Docker, Kubernetes) for scalable applications.
5. Collaboration
   - Work with developers, security teams, and business stakeholders.

Skills Needed to Become a Cloud Infrastructure Engineer

- ✓ Cloud Platforms: AWS, Azure, or Google Cloud
- ✓ Networking & Security: VPNs, Firewalls, Subnets, IAM
- ✓ Scripting & Automation: Python, Bash, PowerShell
- ✓ Infrastructure as Code (IaC): Terraform, CloudFormation
- ✓ Containers & Orchestration: Docker, Kubernetes
- ✓ Monitoring & Logging: CloudWatch, Prometheus, ELK Stack

How to Start as a Student?

1. Learn Cloud Basics: Take free courses on AWS/Azure/GCP.
2. Get Certified: Start with AWS Certified Cloud Practitioner or Microsoft Azure Fundamentals.
3. Hands-on Practice: Use free-tier cloud accounts to deploy projects.
4. Learn DevOps Tools: Git, Docker, Terraform, CI/CD pipelines.
5. Internships & Projects: Work on cloud-related projects or internships.

Career Growth

You can progress to roles like:

- Cloud Architect
- DevOps Engineer
- Site Reliability Engineer (SRE)

Salary: $123,000 to $183,000 Annually

Timeline of Certification: 25 to 40 hours of required study time-four to five hours per day or four weeks consecutively Salary

35 Cloud Compliance Specialist

As a student exploring career options, a Cloud Compliance Specialist might be an interesting role to consider if you're interested in cloud computing, cybersecurity, and regulatory compliance. Here's a breakdown of what this job entails:

What is a Cloud Compliance Specialist?

A Cloud Compliance Specialist ensures that an organization's cloud computing environment follows industry regulations, security standards, and legal requirements. They work with cloud platforms (like AWS, Azure, or Google Cloud) to make sure data is stored, processed, and transmitted securely while meeting compliance frameworks like:

- GDPR (General Data Protection Regulation) – for data privacy in the EU
- HIPAA (Health Insurance Portability and Accountability Act) – for healthcare data in the US
- SOC 2 (Service Organization Control 2) – for security and data protection
- ISO 27001 – for information security management
- PCI DSS (Payment Card Industry Data Security Standard) – for handling credit card data

Key Responsibilities:

1. Auditing & Monitoring – Checking cloud systems for compliance risks.
2. Policy Implementation – Ensuring cloud setups follow security best practices.
3. Risk Assessment – Identifying vulnerabilities in cloud infrastructure.
4. Documentation – Keeping records for audits and legal requirements.
5. Collaboration – Working with IT, legal, and security teams to enforce compliance.

Skills Needed:

- ✓ Cloud Knowledge (AWS/Azure/GCP compliance tools)
- ✓ Understanding of Security Frameworks (GDPR, HIPAA, SOC 2, etc.)
- ✓ Risk Management & Auditing
- ✓ Cybersecurity Basics (Encryption, IAM, Firewalls)
- ✓ Analytical & Communication Skills

How to Become One (as a Student):

1. Learn Cloud Basics – Take free courses on AWS, Azure, or Google Cloud.
2. Study Compliance Standards – Explore GDPR, HIPAA, or SOC 2.
3. Get Certified – Consider certifications like:
   - AWS Certified Security – Specialty
   - Microsoft Certified: Azure Security Engineer
   - Certified Information Systems Auditor (CISA)

4. Gain Experience – Internships in IT security or cloud roles help.

5. Stay Updated – Follow cloud security trends and regulations.

Career Path & Salary:

- Entry-Level: Cloud Security Analyst, IT Auditor
- Mid-Level: Cloud Compliance Specialist, Cloud Risk Consultant
- Senior-Level: Cloud Compliance Manager, Chief Information Security Officer (CISO)
- Salary: 70,000–70,000–120,000+ (varies by experience & location)

Why Consider This Career?

- High demand due to increasing cloud adoption.
- Mix of tech + legal/regulatory knowledge.
- Good earning potential and career growth.

Software Development & Engineering

36 Backend Developer

As a student, understanding the role of a Backend Developer is a great step if you're interested in web development or software engineering. Here's a simple breakdown:

Who is a Backend Developer?

A backend developer is a programmer who focuses on the server-side of web applications. They work on the logic, databases, APIs, and infrastructure that power the frontend (what users see and interact with).

Key Responsibilities:

1. Server-Side Logic: Writing code that handles business logic, user authentication, and data processing.
2. Databases: Storing, retrieving, and managing data efficiently (e.g., MySQL, PostgreSQL, MongoDB).
3. APIs (Application Programming Interfaces): Creating endpoints that allow the frontend (or mobile apps) to communicate with the backend.
4. Performance & Security: Ensuring the application runs fast, scales well, and is secure from attacks.
5. Deployment & DevOps: Managing servers, cloud services (AWS, Azure), and CI/CD pipelines.

Common Technologies Backend Developers Use:

- Programming Languages: Python, Java, JavaScript (Node.js), Ruby, PHP, C#, Go.
- Frameworks: Django (Python), Spring (Java), Express (Node.js), Ruby on Rails, Laravel (PHP).

- Databases: SQL (MySQL, PostgreSQL) & NoSQL (MongoDB, Redis).
- APIs: RESTful APIs, GraphQL.
- Authentication: OAuth, JWT (JSON Web Tokens).
- Cloud & DevOps: AWS, Docker, Kubernetes, GitHub Actions.

Example Workflow:

1. A user submits a login form (frontend).
2. The backend validates the credentials.
3. The server queries the database to check if the user exists.
4. The backend sends a response (success/failure) to the frontend.

How to Become a Backend Developer (as a Student)?

1. Learn a Backend Language (Start with Python/Node.js).
2. Understand Databases (SQL & NoSQL basics).
3. Build APIs (Try making a simple REST API).
4. Work on Projects (E.g., a blog with user authentication).
5. Learn DevOps Basics (Deploy your app on AWS/Heroku).

Frontend vs Backend vs Full-Stack

- Frontend: Deals with UI/UX (HTML, CSS, JavaScript, React).
- Backend: Deals with servers, databases, and APIs.
- Full-Stack: Does both frontend and backend.

Salary: $102,000 to $229,000 Annually

Timeline of Certification: 25 to 40 hours of required study time-four to five hours per day or four weeks consecutively Salary

37 Frontend Developer

As a student, understanding what a Frontend Developer does can help you explore career paths in web development. Here's a simple breakdown:

Who is a Frontend Developer?

A frontend developer builds and designs the visible part of a website or web app—the part users interact with directly (like buttons, forms, animations, and layouts). They focus on user experience (UX) and ensure the site looks good and works well on all devices.

Key Responsibilities:

1. Coding the UI – Turning design mockups (from tools like Figma) into functional code.
2. Making it Interactive – Adding logic for features like search bars, dropdown menus, etc.
3. Optimizing Performance – Ensuring fast loading and smooth animations.
4. Responsive Design – Making sure the site works on phones, tablets, and desktops.
5. Cross-Browser Testing – Fixing issues so the site works on Chrome, Safari, Firefox, etc.

Core Technologies:

1. HTML – Structures the content (text, images, etc.).
2. CSS – Styles the layout (colors, fonts, spacing).
3. JavaScript (JS) – Adds interactivity (e.g., pop-ups, dynamic content).
4. Frameworks/Libraries (Optional but important for jobs):
   o React.js (Most popular)

o   Vue.js or Angular

o   Tailwind CSS (For faster styling)

Bonus Skills (To Stand Out):

- Version Control (Git/GitHub) – For collaboration.
- APIs & HTTP Requests – Fetching data from servers.
- Basic Backend Knowledge (e.g., Node.js, databases).
- UI/UX Principles – To work better with designers.

Career Path:

1. Learn Basics (HTML, CSS, JS) → Build small projects.
2. Learn a Framework (React, Vue, or Angular).
3. Create a Portfolio (Showcase projects on GitHub).
4. Apply for Internships/Junior Roles.

Salary (Globally):

- Junior: 50k–50k–80k/year
- Senior: 90k–90k–130k/year

(Varies by country/company.)

38 Full-Stack Developer

A Full-Stack Developer is a software engineer who can work on both the front-end (client-side) and back-end (server-side) of web applications. They have a broad skill set that allows them to build complete web applications from scratch.

What Does a Full-Stack Developer Do?

1. Front-End Development (What users see & interact with)
    o   Builds user interfaces (UI) using HTML, CSS, JavaScript.
    o   Uses frameworks like React.js, Angular, or Vue.js.
    o   Ensures the website is responsive (works on mobile & desktop).
2. Back-End Development (Server, Database, Logic)
    o   Writes server-side code using languages like Python (Django/Flask), JavaScript (Node.js), Ruby (Ruby on Rails), Java, PHP, or C#.
    o   Manages databases like MySQL, PostgreSQL, MongoDB.
    o   Handles authentication, APIs, and security.
3. DevOps & Deployment (Making the app live)
    o   Works with cloud services (AWS, Azure, Google Cloud).
    o   Uses Docker, Kubernetes for containerization.
    o   Deploys apps using Git, CI/CD pipelines.

Skills Needed to Become a Full-Stack Developer

Category	Technologies
Front-End	HTML, CSS, JavaScript, React, Angular, Vue.js
Back-End	Node.js, Python (Django/Flask), Ruby, Java, PHP
Database	SQL (MySQL, PostgreSQL), NoSQL (MongoDB)
Version Control	Git, GitHub/GitLab
APIs	REST, GraphQL
DevOps	Docker, AWS, CI/CD

Why Become a Full-Stack Developer?

High Demand – Companies prefer developers who can handle both front-end and back-end.

Good Salary – Full-stack devs earn well (varies by experience & location).

Flexibility – Can work on different parts of a project.

Career Growth – Can transition into roles like DevOps, Solution Architect, or Tech Lead.

How to Start as a Student?

1. Learn Basics: HTML, CSS, JavaScript.
2. Pick a Back-End Language: Start with Node.js (JavaScript) or Python.
3. Build Projects: Create a portfolio (e.g., a blog, e-commerce site).
4. Learn Databases: SQL (PostgreSQL) or NoSQL (MongoDB).
5. Explore Frameworks: React (front-end) + Express.js (back-end).
6. Deploy a Project: Use Netlify, Vercel, or Heroku.
7. Salary: $117,000 to $305,000 Annually
8. Timeline of Certification: 25 to 40 hours of required study time- four to five hours per day or four weeks consecutively Salary

39 Mobile Developer

As a student, if you're curious about mobile development, here's a simple breakdown of what a Mobile Developer is and what they do:

Who is a Mobile Developer?

A Mobile Developer is a software engineer who specializes in creating applications (apps) for mobile devices like smartphones and tablets. They build apps for platforms like:

- iOS (Apple iPhones/iPads)
- Android (Samsung, Google Pixel, etc.)
- Sometimes cross-platform (works on both iOS & Android)

What Does a Mobile Developer Do?

1. Design & Build Apps – They write code to make apps functional and user-friendly.
2. Fix Bugs & Improve Performance – They solve problems and optimize apps for speed.
3. Work with UI/UX Designers – They ensure the app looks good and is easy to use.
4. Publish Apps – They upload apps to stores like the Apple App Store or Google Play Store.

Types of Mobile Developers

1. iOS Developer → Uses Swift or Objective-C (for Apple devices).
2. Android Developer → Uses Kotlin or Java (for Android devices).
3. Cross-Platform Developer → Uses frameworks like Flutter (Dart) or React Native (JavaScript) to build apps for both iOS & Android at once.

How to Become a Mobile Developer? (For Students)

- Learn Programming Basics (Start with Python, JavaScript, or Java).
- Pick a Platform (iOS, Android, or Cross-Platform).
- Take Online Courses (Udemy, Coursera, freeCodeCamp).
- Build Small Projects (To-do app, weather app, etc.).
- Publish an App (Great for your portfolio!).

Why Become a Mobile Developer?

High demand for app developers.

Good salary (even for entry-level jobs).

Fun & creative work.

You can build your own apps and startups!

Salary: $102,000 to $229,000 Annually

Timeline of Certification: 25 to 40 hours of required study time-four to five hours per day or four weeks consecutively Salary

40 Embedded Systems Engineer

An Embedded Systems Engineer is a professional who designs, develops, and maintains embedded systems—specialized computing systems that perform dedicated functions within larger mechanical or electrical systems. These systems are found in everyday devices like smartphones, cars, medical equipment, home appliances, and industrial machines.

Key Responsibilities of an Embedded Systems Engineer:

1. Hardware-Software Integration
   - Works with microcontrollers (e.g., ARM, AVR, PIC) and microprocessors.
   - Interfaces sensors, actuators, and communication modules (Wi-Fi, Bluetooth, UART, SPI, I2C).
2. Firmware Development
   - Writes low-level code (C, C++, Rust, or Assembly) to control hardware.
   - Optimizes for performance, power efficiency, and real-time constraints.
3. Debugging & Testing
   - Uses oscilloscopes, logic analyzers, and debuggers to troubleshoot issues.
   - Performs unit testing and validation.

4. RTOS (Real-Time Operating Systems)
   o Works with real-time schedulers (FreeRTOS, Zephyr, VxWorks) for time-critical applications.
5. PCB Design (Sometimes)
   o May design or review circuit schematics and layouts (using tools like Altium, KiCad).

Skills Required:

- ✓ Programming: C/C++ (most important), Python (for scripting)
- ✓ Microcontrollers: STM32, Arduino, ESP32, Raspberry Pi Pico
- ✓ Protocols: UART, I2C, SPI, CAN, USB, Ethernet
- ✓ RTOS & Bare-Metal Programming
- ✓ Debugging Tools: JTAG, GDB, Logic Analyzers
- ✓ Basic Electronics: ADC, PWM, GPIO, Timers

Career Path for Students:

- Learn Basics: Start with Arduino/Raspberry Pi projects.
- Study Electronics: Understand circuits, sensors, and communication protocols.
- Master C Programming: Embedded systems rely heavily on efficient C code.
- Explore RTOS: Try FreeRTOS on an STM32 board.
- Internships: Work with IoT, automotive, or robotics companies.

Industries Hiring Embedded Engineers:

- Automotive (Self-driving cars, ECUs)
- Consumer Electronics (Smart devices, wearables)
- Medical Devices (Pacemakers, imaging systems)
- Aerospace & Defense (Drones, avionics)
- Industrial Automation (Robotics, PLCs)

Salary Expectations (Varies by Region & Experience):

- Entry-Level: 60,000–60,000–90,000/year
- Experienced: 100,000–100,000–181,000+

41 Game Developer

A game developer is a professional who designs, programs, and creates video games for various platforms like PCs, consoles, mobile devices, and VR/AR systems. Game development involves multiple roles, including:

1. Game Designers
   - Come up with game concepts, rules, and mechanics.
   - Design levels, characters, and storylines.
2. Programmers (Game Developers in a technical sense)
   - Write code to make the game work (using languages like C++, C#, Python, etc.).
   - Work on physics, AI, gameplay, and networking.
3. Artists & Animators
   - Create 2D/3D models, textures, and animations.
   - Use tools like Blender, Maya, or Photoshop.
4. Sound Designers & Composers
   - Make sound effects, background music, and voiceovers.
5. Testers (QA)
   - Find and report bugs to improve the game before release.

How to Become a Game Developer as a Student?

- Learn Programming (Start with C# for Unity or C++ for Unreal Engine).
- Use Game Engines (Try Unity, Unreal Engine, or Godot).

- Make Small Games (Start with simple projects like Pong or Flappy Bird).
- Join Game Jams (Events where you make a game in a short time).
- Study Math & Physics (Helpful for game mechanics).
- Build a Portfolio (Showcase your projects on GitHub or Itch.io).
- Salary: $56,000 to $1732,000 Annually
- Timeline of Certification: 25 to 40 hours of required study time- four to five hours per day or four weeks consecutively Salary

42 API developer

As a student exploring career options, you might be curious about what an API Developer does. Let me break it down simply:

What is an API Developer?

An API (Application Programming Interface) Developer is a software engineer who designs, builds, and maintains APIs—the "bridges" that allow different software systems to communicate with each other.

For example:

- When you use a weather app, it fetches data from a weather service via an API.
- When you log in to a website using Google or Facebook, that's also done through an API.

What Does an API Developer Do?

1. Design APIs – Decide how different systems will interact (REST, GraphQL, SOAP).

2. Develop APIs – Write code (often in Python, JavaScript, Java, or C#) to create APIs.

3. Test APIs – Ensure they work correctly, handle errors, and are secure.

4. Document APIs – Write clear instructions so other developers can use them.

5. Optimize APIs – Make them fast, scalable, and efficient.

Skills Needed to Become an API Developer

- Programming Languages: Python, JavaScript (Node.js), Java, or C#.
- API Protocols: REST (most common), GraphQL, gRPC, SOAP.
- Frameworks/Tools: Express.js (Node), Flask/Django (Python), Postman (testing).
- Authentication: OAuth, JWT (for security).
- Database Knowledge: SQL (PostgreSQL, MySQL) or NoSQL (MongoDB).
- Cloud Services: AWS, Azure, or Google Cloud (for deploying APIs).

Why Become an API Developer?

High Demand: APIs power modern apps (mobile, web, IoT), so companies always need API devs.
Good Salary: Entry-level API developers earn well (varies by location).
Versatile Role: You'll work with frontend, backend, and cloud technologies.

How to Start as a Student?

1. Learn a Programming Language (Python or JavaScript is beginner-friendly).

2. Build Simple APIs (Try making a weather API or a to-do list API).

3. Use Postman to test APIs.
4. Explore Open-Source Projects (GitHub has many API projects).
5. Internships & Freelancing – Gain real-world experience.

Salary: $90,000 to $108,000 Annually

Timeline of Certification: 25 to 40 hours of required study time-four to five hours per day or four weeks consecutively Salary

43 Microservices Developer

As a student exploring career paths in software development, you might be curious about what a Microservices Developer does. Let me break it down in simple terms:

Who is a Microservices Developer?

A Microservices Developer is a software engineer who designs, builds, and maintains applications using the microservices architecture. Instead of creating one big, monolithic application, they break it down into smaller, independent services that communicate with each other.

Key Responsibilities

1. Designing Microservices – Breaking down a large application into smaller, loosely coupled services.
2. Developing APIs – Creating RESTful or gRPC APIs for services to communicate.
3. Using Cloud & Containers – Deploying services using Docker, Kubernetes, or cloud platforms (AWS, Azure, GCP).

4. Database Management – Decentralizing databases (each service may have its own database).

5. Ensuring Scalability & Fault Tolerance – Making sure services can scale independently and handle failures.

6. Implementing CI/CD – Automating deployments using DevOps tools (Jenkins, GitHub Actions).

7. Monitoring & Logging – Using tools like Prometheus, Grafana, or ELK Stack to track performance.

Skills Required

- Programming Languages: Java (Spring Boot), Python (FastAPI), Go, Node.js, or .NET Core.
- APIs & Protocols: REST, GraphQL, gRPC, WebSockets.
- Databases: SQL (PostgreSQL, MySQL) & NoSQL (MongoDB, Cassandra).
- Cloud & DevOps: Docker, Kubernetes, AWS/Azure, CI/CD pipelines.
- Messaging Systems: Kafka, RabbitMQ (for async communication).
- Testing & Security: Unit testing, integration testing, OAuth, JWT.

Why Become a Microservices Developer?

- High demand in modern cloud-based applications.
- Better scalability and maintainability than monolithic apps.
- Exposure to cutting-edge technologies (cloud, DevOps, containers).
- Good salary prospects (one of the well-paid roles in software engineering).

How to Start as a Student?

1. Learn a backend language (Java/Spring Boot or Python).
2. Build small REST APIs and deploy them.

3. Learn Docker & Kubernetes basics.

4. Explore cloud platforms (AWS/Azure free tiers).

5. Contribute to open-source microservices projects.

Salary: $90,000 to $151,000 Annually

Timeline of Certification: 25 to 40 hours of required study time-four to five hours per day or four weeks consecutively Salary

44 Blockchain Developer

A Blockchain Developer is a specialized software engineer who builds decentralized applications (DApps), smart contracts, and protocols using blockchain technology. Blockchain developers work on distributed ledger systems like Bitcoin, Ethereum, Solana, and Hyperledger to create secure, transparent, and tamper-proof solutions.

Types of Blockchain Developers:

1. Core Blockchain Developer
   - Works on the underlying blockchain protocol (e.g., improving Bitcoin or Ethereum).
   - Focuses on consensus mechanisms, cryptography, and network security.
   - Requires deep knowledge of C++, Rust, or Go.

2. Smart Contract / DApp Developer
   - Builds decentralized applications (DApps) and smart contracts.
   - Works with platforms like Ethereum, Solana, or Polkadot.
   - Uses languages like Solidity (Ethereum), Rust (Solana), or Vyper.

Skills Required to Become a Blockchain Developer:

- Programming Languages: Solidity, JavaScript, Python, Rust, Go.
- Blockchain Platforms: Ethereum, Binance Smart Chain, Hyperledger, Polkadot.
- Smart Contracts: Writing & deploying secure contracts.
- Web3.js / Ethers.js: Interacting with blockchain via frontend.
- Cryptography: Understanding of hashing, digital signatures, and consensus (PoW, PoS).
- Decentralized Storage: IPFS, Filecoin.
- Tools: Truffle, Hardhat, Remix IDE, MetaMask.

How to Start as a Student?

1. Learn Basics of Blockchain (How blocks, hashes, and consensus work).
2. Master a Programming Language (JavaScript/Python → Solidity/ Rust).
3. Build Simple Smart Contracts (Try Remix IDE or Hardhat).
4. Explore Ethereum & Web3.js (Create a basic DApp).
5. Join Blockchain Communities (GitHub, Ethereum forums, Discord groups).
6. Contribute to Open-Source Projects (GitHub repositories).

Career Opportunities:

- Blockchain Engineer
- Smart Contract Auditor (Security-focused)
- Web3 Developer
- DeFi (Decentralized Finance) Developer
- NFT & Gaming Developer

Salary Expectations (Globally):

- Entry-Level: 70,000–70,000–120,000/year
- Experienced: 150,000–150,000–250,000+

45 Rust Developer

A Rust Developer is a software engineer who specializes in writing applications, systems, or tools using the Rust programming language. Rust is a modern, high-performance language known for its focus on memory safety, concurrency, and zero-cost abstractions.

What Does a Rust Developer Do?

As a Rust developer, you might:

- Build high-performance systems (like game engines, databases, or operating systems).
- Work on blockchain & Web3 projects (e.g., Solana, Polkadot).
- Develop networking & embedded systems (IoT, robotics).
- Write secure and efficient backend services (web servers, APIs).
- Contribute to open-source projects (like Mozilla, Linux, or Rust itself).

Why Learn Rust as a Student?

High Demand: Companies like Google, Microsoft, and Meta use Rust for critical systems.

Great Salaries: Rust developers are among the highest-paid (often $100K+ for entry-level).

Future-Proof: Rust is growing fast in areas like AI, cloud computing, and cybersecurity.

Strong Community: Rust has a welcoming and helpful community (great for learning).

How to Become a Rust Developer?

1. Learn Rust Basics – Start with The Rust Book.
2. Work on Projects – Build CLI tools, web servers, or contribute to open-source.
3. Master Key Concepts – Ownership, Borrowing, Lifetimes, and Async.
4. Explore Frameworks – Actix (web), Tokio (async), Bevy (game dev).
5. Apply for Internships/Jobs – Look for roles in fintech, blockchain, or systems programming.

Career Paths for Rust Developers

- Systems Programmer (OS, compilers, embedded)
- Backend Engineer (high-performance APIs)
- Blockchain Developer (Solana, Ethereum, Cosmos)
- DevOps/Tooling Engineer (build fast, reliable tools)

46 Golang Developer

A Golang Developer is a software engineer who specializes in using the Go programming language (also known as Golang) to build efficient, scalable, and reliable software applications.

What Does a Golang Developer Do?

As a Golang Developer, you would:

1. Write clean and efficient code using Go for backend systems, APIs, microservices, and cloud-based applications.
2. Work with databases (SQL & NoSQL) to store and retrieve data.
3. Develop high-performance systems (e.g., web servers, distributed systems, networking tools).
4. Use Go frameworks & tools like Gin, Echo, Beego, or Gorilla for web development.
5. Deploy applications using Docker, Kubernetes, and cloud platforms (AWS, GCP, Azure).
6. Optimize code for speed, scalability, and concurrency (Go is great for handling multiple tasks at once).

Why Become a Golang Developer?

High Demand – Companies like Google, Uber, Twitch, and Docker use Go.
Fast & Scalable – Go is great for cloud computing and microservices.
Easy to Learn – Simpler syntax compared to C++ or Java.
Great Salary – Golang developers are well-paid due to high demand.

How to Become a Golang Developer as a Student?

1. Learn Go Basics – Start with A Tour of Go (official tutorial).
2. Build Projects – Create CLI tools, REST APIs, or a simple web server.
3. Learn Concurrency – Master goroutines and channels (Go's superpower!).
4. Explore Frameworks – Try Gin or Echo for web development.
5. Contribute to Open Source – Check out GitHub projects in Go.

6. Apply for Internships – Many companies hire junior Golang developers.

Salary: $96,000 to $141,000 Annually

Timeline of Certification: 25 to 40 hours of required study time-four to five hours per day or four weeks consecutively Salary

47. Python Developer

A Python Developer is a software developer who specializes in writing, testing, and maintaining code using the Python programming language. Python is widely used in web development, data science, automation, artificial intelligence (AI), and more.

What Does a Python Developer Do?

1. Writing Code – Developing applications, scripts, or tools using Python.
2. Debugging & Testing – Finding and fixing errors in Python programs.
3. Working with Frameworks – Using Python frameworks like:
    o   Django or Flask (for web development)
    o   Pandas, NumPy (for data analysis)
    o   TensorFlow, PyTorch (for AI/ML)
4. APIs & Integrations – Connecting Python apps to databases (like PostgreSQL, MySQL) or external services.
5. Automation – Writing scripts to automate repetitive tasks.
6. Collaboration – Working with teams using Git and agile methodologies.

Skills Needed to Become a Python Developer

- Strong knowledge of Python syntax & libraries
- Understanding of OOP (Object-Oriented Programming)
- Basics of front-end (HTML, CSS, JavaScript) for web development
- Knowledge of databases (SQL/NoSQL)
- Familiarity with Git & GitHub
- Problem-solving & logical thinking

How to Start as a Student?

1. Learn Python Basics – Variables, loops, functions, data structures (lists, dictionaries).
2. Build Small Projects – A calculator, to-do app, or a simple web scraper.
3. Explore Python Libraries – Try Pandas for data or Flask for web apps.
4. Contribute to Open Source – Check GitHub for Python projects.
5. Internships & Freelancing – Gain real-world experience.

Career Paths for Python Developers

- Web Developer (Django/Flask)
- Data Scientist/Analyst (Pandas, NumPy)
- Machine Learning Engineer (TensorFlow, Scikit-learn)
- DevOps/Automation Engineer (Scripting, CI/CD)

Salary: $78,000 to $150,000 Annually

Timeline of Certification: 25 to 40 hours of required study time-four to five hours per day or four weeks consecutively Salary

48 Java Developer

As a student, if you're curious about what a Java Developer is, here's a simple breakdown:

Who is a Java Developer?

A Java Developer is a software engineer who specializes in using the Java programming language to build applications, websites, and systems. Java is one of the most popular programming languages, used in:

- Web applications (backend services)
- Mobile apps (Android development)
- Enterprise software (banking, e-commerce)
- Big Data & Cloud computing (Hadoop, AWS)
- Game development (Minecraft was built in Java!)

What Does a Java Developer Do?

A Java Developer typically:

- ✓ Writes, tests, and debugs Java code
- ✓ Works with frameworks like Spring, Hibernate, Jakarta EE
- ✓ Builds APIs and microservices
- ✓ Uses databases like MySQL, PostgreSQL, MongoDB
- ✓ Collaborates with frontend developers (who work with JavaScript/ React)
- ✓ Deploys applications on servers (like Tomcat, Docker, Kubernetes)

Skills Needed to Become a Java Developer

1. Core Java (OOP, Collections, Multithreading)
2. Java Frameworks (Spring Boot, Jakarta EE)

3. Database & SQL (MySQL, PostgreSQL)
4. Tools (Maven, Git, IntelliJ IDEA/Eclipse)
5. Web Technologies (REST APIs, HTTP, JSON/XML)
6. Basic DevOps (Docker, Jenkins, AWS)

How to Start as a Student?

- Learn Core Java first (variables, loops, OOP concepts)
- Practice coding on HackerRank, LeetCode
- Build small projects (e.g., a Student Management System)
- Learn Spring Boot (most in-demand Java framework)
- Contribute to open-source projects on GitHub
- Apply for internships in software companies

Career & Salary

- Entry-Level Java Developer: 60K–60K–90K/year (varies by country)
- Experienced Developer: 100K–100K–150K+
- Roles: Backend Developer, Android Developer, Software Engineer

Why Choose Java?

High demand in enterprises

Strong community support

Platform-independent (Write Once, Run

Salary: $117,000 to $148,000 Annually

Timeline of Certification: 25 to 40 hours of required study time-four to five hours per day or four weeks consecutively Salary

49 C++ Developer

A C++ Developer is a software engineer who specializes in writing, testing, and maintaining code using the C++ programming language. C++ is a powerful, high-performance language commonly used in systems programming, game development, embedded systems, and performance-critical applications.

What Does a C++ Developer Do?

As a C++ developer, you would typically:

1. Write and optimize C++ code for applications, games, operating systems, or embedded systems.
2. Debug and fix issues in existing C++ programs.
3. Work with memory management (since C++ allows manual memory control).
4. Develop algorithms for high-performance computing.
5. Use libraries like STL (Standard Template Library) and frameworks like Boost.
6. Collaborate with teams on large-scale software projects.
7. Work on cross-platform development (Windows, Linux, macOS, etc.).
8. Integrate C++ with other languages (like Python or Java via APIs).

Industries Hiring C++ Developers

- Game Development (Unreal Engine, game engines)
- System Software (Operating systems, drivers)
- Finance & Trading Systems (High-frequency trading)
- Embedded Systems (IoT, robotics, automotive)
- AI & Machine Learning (Performance-critical components)

- Telecommunications & Networking

Skills Needed to Become a C++ Developer

1. Strong C++ knowledge (C++11/14/17/20 standards)
2. Understanding of OOP & memory management
3. Data structures & algorithms
4. Multithreading & concurrency
5. Debugging & performance optimization
6. Familiarity with build systems (CMake, Make)
7. Version control (Git)
8. Knowledge of operating systems & hardware

How to Start as a Student?

- Learn C++ basics (syntax, pointers, OOP).
- Practice on LeetCode, Codeforces, or HackerRank.
- Contribute to open-source C++ projects (GitHub).
- Build small projects (e.g., a game, a compiler, or a system tool).
- Explore Unreal Engine (if interested in game dev).
- Intern at companies using C++ (e.g., gaming, embedded systems).

Career Growth

- Junior C++ Developer → Senior C++ Engineer → Lead/Architect
- Can transition into Game Dev, Systems Programming, or High-Performance Computing.

Salary: $74,000 to $231,000 Annually

Timeline of Certification: 25 to 40 hours of required study time-four to five hours per day or four weeks consecutively Salary

50 Scala Developer

As a student, you might be curious about what a Scala Developer is and what they do. Let me break it down for you in simple terms:

Who is a Scala Developer?

A Scala Developer is a software engineer who specializes in writing code using the Scala programming language. Scala is a powerful, high-level language that combines object-oriented and functional programming concepts. It runs on the Java Virtual Machine (JVM), meaning it can interoperate with Java libraries.

What Does a Scala Developer Do?

A Scala Developer typically works on:

1. Backend Development – Building server-side applications (e.g., APIs, microservices).
2. Big Data & Distributed Systems – Using frameworks like Apache Spark, Akka, Kafka.
3. Web Development – Using Scala-based frameworks like Play Framework.
4. Data Engineering & Analytics – Processing large datasets efficiently.
5. Financial & Trading Systems – Many banks and fintech companies use Scala for high-performance computing.

Skills Required to Become a Scala Developer

1. Strong Scala Knowledge – Understanding of functional programming, case classes, pattern matching, etc.
2. JVM Ecosystem – Familiarity with Java libraries and tools.

3. Big Data Tools – Experience with Spark, Hadoop, Flink (if working in data engineering).
4. Concurrency & Parallelism – Knowledge of Akka, Futures, ZIO.
5. Build Tools – sbt (Scala Build Tool), Maven, Gradle.
6. Databases – SQL (PostgreSQL, MySQL) & NoSQL (MongoDB, Cassandra).
7. Testing Frameworks – ScalaTest, Specs2.

Why Learn Scala as a Student?

- High Demand – Used in big tech companies (Twitter, LinkedIn, Netflix, Databricks).
- Good Salaries – Scala developers are often well-paid due to niche expertise.
- Functional Programming Skills – Helps in learning other languages like Haskell, Rust, or F#.
- Big Data & AI – Scala + Spark is widely used in data science and machine learning pipelines.

How to Start Learning Scala?

1. Learn Basics – Install Scala, use Scala REPL, try simple programs.
2. Online Courses – Coursera, Udemy, Rock the JVM (great for Scala).
3. Books – Programming in Scala (by Martin Odersky, the creator of Scala).
4. Build Projects – Try small apps, contribute to open-source Scala projects.
5. Join Communities – Scala Discord, Reddit, Stack Overflow.

Career Path for a Scala Developer

- Junior Scala Developer → Senior Scala Engineer
- Big Data Engineer (Spark Specialist)
- Tech Lead / Architect
- Research & Development (Functional Programming)

Companies Hiring Scala Developers

- Tech: Twitter, LinkedIn, Netflix, Spotify
- Finance: Goldman Sachs, Morgan Stanley, Barclays
- Big Data: Databricks, Palantir

Final Advice

If you enjoy functional programming, distributed systems, or big data, Scala is a great language to learn. Start with small projects, explore frameworks like Akka/Play, and consider contributing to open-source Scala projects to build experience.

Salary: $117,000 to $172,000 Annually

Timeline of Certification: 25 to 40 hours of required study time-four to five hours per day or four weeks consecutively Salary

Data & AI/ML Remote Jobs

51 Data Engineer

As a student, understanding the role of a Data Engineer can be very useful, especially if you're interested in data, programming, or technology. Here's a simple breakdown:

Who is a Data Engineer?

A Data Engineer is a professional who designs, builds, and maintains the systems and infrastructure that allow organizations to collect, store, process, and analyze large amounts of data. They ensure that data is reliable, accessible, and optimized for data scientists, analysts, and business users.

Key Responsibilities of a Data Engineer

1. Building Data Pipelines
   - Creating systems to move data from different sources (databases, APIs, logs) to storage (like data warehouses/lakes).
2. Database Management
   - Designing and maintaining databases (SQL & NoSQL) for efficient data storage and retrieval.
3. ETL (Extract, Transform, Load) Processes
   - Cleaning, transforming, and structuring raw data into usable formats.
4. Big Data Technologies
   - Working with tools like Hadoop, Spark, Kafka to handle large-scale data processing.
5. Cloud & Infrastructure
   - Using cloud platforms (AWS, GCP, Azure) to manage scalable data systems.

6. Data Security & Compliance
   - Ensuring data privacy, security, and compliance with regulations (GDPR, HIPAA).
7. Collaboration with Data Teams
   - Supporting data scientists and analysts by providing clean, structured data.

Skills Required

- Programming: Python, Java, Scala, SQL
- Databases: PostgreSQL, MySQL, MongoDB, Cassandra
- Big Data Tools: Hadoop, Spark, Kafka
- Cloud Platforms: AWS (S3, Redshift), Google BigQuery, Azure Data Lake
- ETL Tools: Apache Airflow, Talend, Informatica
- Version Control: Git, GitHub

How is a Data Engineer Different From a Data Scientist?

- Data Engineers focus on infrastructure & pipelines (moving and storing data).
- Data Scientists focus on analyzing data (machine learning, statistics, insights).

Why Become a Data Engineer?
- High demand & good salaries 💰
- Work with cutting-edge tech (AI/ML, Big Data, Cloud) ☁️
- Foundation for roles like Data Scientist, ML Engineer, or Analytics Engineer

How to Start as a Student?

1. Learn SQL & Python (most important!).
2. Work on projects (build a data pipeline, scrape & store data).
3. Explore cloud platforms (AWS/GCP free tiers).
4. Take online courses (Coursera, Udemy, YouTube).
5. Internships or open-source contributions.

Salary: $114,000 to $162,000 Annually

Timeline of Certification: 25 to 40 hours of required study time-four to five hours per day or four weeks consecutively Salary

52 Data Scientist

As a student, it's great that you're curious about Data Science! A Data Scientist is a professional who uses data analysis, statistics, machine learning, and programming to extract insights from large datasets. They help businesses and organizations make data-driven decisions.

What Does a Data Scientist Do?

1. Collect & Clean Data – Gather data from databases, APIs, or web scraping, then clean and organize it.
2. Analyze Data – Use statistical methods to find trends, patterns, and correlations.
3. Build Machine Learning Models – Develop predictive models using algorithms like regression, decision trees, or neural networks.
4. Visualize Data – Create charts, graphs, and dashboards (using tools like Tableau, Matplotlib, or Power BI).

5. Communicate Insights – Explain findings to non-technical stakeholders through reports or presentations.

Skills Needed to Become a Data Scientist

Programming – Python (most common) or R
Statistics & Math – Probability, linear algebra, hypothesis testing
Data Manipulation – SQL, Pandas, NumPy
Machine Learning – Scikit-learn, TensorFlow, PyTorch
Data Visualization – Matplotlib, Seaborn, Tableau
Big Data Tools (Optional) – Hadoop, Spark (for large datasets)

How to Start as a Student?

1. Learn Python/R – Take online courses (Coursera, Udemy, freeCodeCamp).
2. Practice SQL – Work with databases (try LeetCode or HackerRank).
3. Study Statistics – Khan Academy or university courses.
4. Do Projects – Analyze datasets from Kaggle, build a small ML model.
5. Join Competitions – Participate in Kaggle challenges.
6. Internships – Apply for data-related roles to gain experience.

Career Paths in Data Science

- Data Analyst (Entry-level, focuses on reporting & visualization)
- Machine Learning Engineer (Builds AI models)
- Data Engineer (Handles data pipelines & infrastructure)
- Business Intelligence (BI) Analyst (Works with dashboards & KPIs)

Salary: $90,000 to $165,000 Annually

Timeline of Certification: 25 to 40 hours of required study time-four to five hours per day or four weeks consecutively

53 Machine Learning Engineer

As a student, you might be curious about careers in tech, and Machine Learning (ML) Engineer is one of the most exciting roles in artificial intelligence (AI). Here's a simple breakdown:

What is a Machine Learning Engineer?

An ML Engineer is a professional who designs, builds, and deploys machine learning models to solve real-world problems. They work at the intersection of software engineering and data science, turning data into intelligent systems.

Key Responsibilities:

1. Developing ML Models – Creating algorithms that learn from data (e.g., recommendation systems, image recognition, chatbots).
2. Data Processing – Cleaning and preparing data for training models.
3. Model Training & Optimization – Improving accuracy and efficiency.
4. Deployment – Integrating models into apps, websites, or services (e.g., using cloud platforms like AWS, GCP).
5. Monitoring & Maintenance – Ensuring models perform well over time.

Skills Required:

- ✓ Programming – Python (most common), R, C++
- ✓ ML Frameworks – TensorFlow, PyTorch, Scikit-learn
- ✓ Mathematics – Statistics, Linear Algebra, Calculus
- ✓ Data Handling – SQL, Pandas, NumPy

✓ Software Engineering – APIs, Docker, CI/CD
✓ Problem-Solving – Ability to design efficient AI solutions

How to Become an ML Engineer? (For Students)

1. Learn Basics – Start with Python and math fundamentals.
2. Take Online Courses – (e.g., Coursera's ML by Andrew Ng, Fast.ai).
3. Work on Projects – Build simple models (e.g., spam detector, stock predictor).
4. Compete in Hackathons/Kaggle – Gain practical experience.
5. Internships/Open Source – Work with real-world data.
6. Advanced Studies (Optional) – A degree in CS/AI helps but isn't mandatory.

Salary & Job Outlook

Average Salary (Global): 100K–100K–150K (varies by location/ experience).
High Demand – Industries like tech, healthcare, finance, and robotics need ML Engineers.

ML Engineer vs Data Scientist

• Data Scientists focus more on analysis and insights.
• ML Engineers focus on building and deploying scalable models.

Salary: $53,000 to $232,000 Annually

Timeline of Certification: 25 to 40 hours of required study time-four to five hours per day or four weeks consecutively

54. AI Research Scientist

An AI Research Scientist is a professional who conducts research to advance the field of Artificial Intelligence (AI). They develop new algorithms, models, and techniques to improve machine learning, deep learning, natural language processing (NLP), computer vision, robotics, and other AI-related domains.

What Does an AI Research Scientist Do?

1. Research & Development (R&D)
   - Work on cutting-edge AI problems (e.g., improving large language models like GPT, reinforcement learning, or AI ethics).
   - Publish papers in top conferences (NeurIPS, ICML, CVPR, ACL, etc.).
2. Algorithm Design & Optimization
   - Develop new machine learning models (e.g., transformers, diffusion models).
   - Improve efficiency, scalability, and robustness of AI systems.
3. Experiment & Implementation
   - Train and fine-tune AI models using frameworks like PyTorch or TensorFlow.
   - Work with large datasets and high-performance computing (GPUs/TPUs).
4. Collaboration
   - Work with engineers to deploy AI models in real-world applications.
   - Partner with universities, tech companies (Google DeepMind, OpenAI, Meta AI), or research labs.

Skills Needed to Become an AI Research Scientist

- ✓ Strong Math & Statistics (Linear Algebra, Calculus, Probability)
- ✓ Programming (Python, PyTorch, TensorFlow, CUDA)
- ✓ Deep Learning & Machine Learning Expertise
- ✓ Research Skills (Reading papers, experimentation, writing)
- ✓ Problem-Solving & Creativity

How to Become One (As a Student)

1. Study AI/ML Fundamentals (Take online courses like Coursera, Fast.ai, or university classes).
2. Work on Research Projects (Join a lab, contribute to open-source AI projects).
3. Read Research Papers (Follow arXiv, Google Scholar).
4. Publish & Present Work (Start with smaller conferences, collaborate with professors).
5. Get a PhD (Optional but Common) – Many AI researchers have a PhD in CS, Math, or related fields.

Career Paths

- Academia (Professor, Research Scientist at a university)
- Industry (Google Brain, OpenAI, NVIDIA, Meta AI, etc.)
- Startups & AI Labs (Working on specialized AI applications)

Salary: $50,000 to $174,000 Annually

Timeline of Certification: 25 to 40 hours of required study time-four to five hours per day or four weeks consecutively

55. Business Intelligence Developer

A Business Intelligence (BI) Developer is a professional who designs, develops, and maintains tools and systems that help businesses analyze data and make data-driven decisions. They work with databases, data warehouses, and BI tools to transform raw data into meaningful insights through reports, dashboards, and visualizations.

Key Responsibilities of a BI Developer:

1. Data Modeling & Warehousing
   - Design and maintain data warehouses (e.g., SQL Server, Snowflake, Redshift).
   - Create schemas (star, snowflake) for efficient data storage and retrieval.
2. ETL (Extract, Transform, Load) Processes
   - Extract data from various sources (databases, APIs, spreadsheets).
   - Clean, transform, and load data into a usable format (using tools like SSIS, Talend, or Python).
3. Report & Dashboard Development
   - Build interactive dashboards (using Power BI, Tableau, Qlik).
   - Develop SQL queries and stored procedures for reporting.
4. Data Analysis & Visualization
   - Identify trends and patterns to support business decisions.
   - Optimize reports for performance and usability.
5. Collaboration with Stakeholders
   - Work with business analysts, managers, and data engineers to understand requirements.
   - Train end-users on BI tools and reports.

Skills Required to Become a BI Developer:

- Technical Skills:
    - SQL (queries, joins, optimization)
    - BI Tools (Power BI, Tableau, Looker)
    - ETL Tools (SSIS, Informatica, Alteryx)
    - Data Warehousing (Snowflake, BigQuery, Redshift)
    - Basic Programming (Python, DAX, R)
- Soft Skills:
    - Analytical thinking
    - Problem-solving
    - Communication (explaining insights to non-technical users)

Career Path for a Student:

1. Learn Fundamentals:
    - Take courses in SQL, data analysis, and BI tools (Coursera, Udemy, freeCodeCamp).
2. Gain Experience:
    - Internships or projects analyzing real-world datasets.
    - Build a portfolio with sample dashboards (e.g., GitHub, personal website).
3. Certifications (Optional but Helpful):
    - Microsoft Certified: Power BI Data Analyst
    - Tableau Desktop Specialist
4. Entry-Level Roles:
    - BI Analyst → BI Developer → Senior BI Developer → Data Engineer/Architect.

Salary Expectations (Varies by Location & Experience):

- Entry-Level: 60,000–60,000–80,000/year (US)
- Experienced: 90,000–90,000–120,000/year

Why Become a BI Developer?

- High demand across industries (finance, healthcare, retail).
- Combines technical skills with business impact.
- Good career growth into data engineering or analytics.

56 Data Analyst

As a student, you might be curious about what a Data Analyst does and whether it could be a good career path for you. Here's a simple breakdown:

What is a Data Analyst?

A Data Analyst is a professional who collects, processes, and analyzes data to help businesses make better decisions. They turn raw data into meaningful insights using tools like Excel, SQL, Python, or visualization tools like Tableau and Power BI.

Key Responsibilities of a Data Analyst:

1. Data Collection – Gathering data from databases, surveys, or web analytics.
2. Data Cleaning – Removing errors and inconsistencies to ensure accuracy.
3. Data Analysis – Using statistical methods to find trends and patterns.
4. Data Visualization – Creating charts, graphs, and dashboards to present findings.
5. Reporting – Summarizing insights for managers or stakeholders to guide decisions.

Skills Needed to Become a Data Analyst:

- ✓ Technical Skills:
    - Excel (for basic analysis)
    - SQL (for database queries)
    - Python/R (for advanced analysis)
    - Tableau/Power BI (for visualization)
    - Statistics (to interpret data)
- ✓ Soft Skills:
    - Problem-solving
    - Attention to detail
    - Communication (explaining insights clearly)

Why Become a Data Analyst?

High demand in industries like finance, healthcare, marketing, and tech.

Good salary (even at entry-level).

Opportunities to grow into roles like Data Scientist or Business Analyst.

How to Start as a Student?

- Learn Excel & SQL (free courses on YouTube, Coursera, or Khan Academy).
- Practice with real datasets (Kaggle, Google Dataset Search).
- Build a portfolio (showcase projects on GitHub or LinkedIn).
- Do internships or freelance projects to gain experience.

Salary: $82,000 to $120,000 Annually

Timeline of Certification: 25 to 40 hours of required study time-four to five hours per day or four weeks consecutively

57 Big Data Engineer

Who is a Big Data Engineer?

A Big Data Engineer is a professional who designs, builds, and manages large-scale data processing systems. They work with massive datasets (structured and unstructured) to ensure data is collected, stored, and analyzed efficiently.

Key Responsibilities:

1. Data Pipeline Development – Building systems to move and process data.
2. Data Storage – Setting up databases (SQL/NoSQL) and data lakes/warehouses.
3. Data Processing – Using tools like Hadoop, Spark, and Kafka.
4. Cloud & Distributed Systems – Working with AWS, Google Cloud, or Azure.
5. Data Optimization – Improving performance and scalability.
6. ETL (Extract, Transform, Load) – Cleaning and preparing data for analysis.

Skills Required:

- ✓ Programming: Python, Java, Scala
- ✓ Big Data Tools: Hadoop, Spark, Kafka, Flink
- ✓ Databases: SQL (PostgreSQL, MySQL), NoSQL (MongoDB, Cassandra)
- ✓ Cloud Platforms: AWS (S3, Redshift), Google Cloud (BigQuery), Azure
- ✓ Data Pipelines: Airflow, Luigi
- ✓ Linux & DevOps Basics (Docker, Kubernetes)

How to Become One (as a Student):

1. Learn Programming (Python/Java).
2. Understand Databases (SQL + NoSQL).
3. Explore Big Data Tools (Hadoop, Spark).
4. Work on Projects (e.g., build a data pipeline).
5. Take Online Courses (Coursera, Udacity, edX).
6. Internships (Look for data engineering roles).

Career Growth:

- Junior Big Data Engineer → Senior → Data Architect
- Can transition into Data Science, Machine Learning Engineering, or Analytics Engineering.

Salary: $59,000 to $229,000 Annually

Timeline of Certification: 25 to 40 hours of required study time-four to five hours per day or four weeks consecutively

58 NLP Engineer

As a student, if you're curious about Natural Language Processing (NLP) Engineering, here's a simple breakdown:

What is an NLP Engineer?

An NLP Engineer is a professional who specializes in developing systems that enable computers to understand, interpret, and generate human language. They work at the intersection of computer science, artificial intelligence (AI), and linguistics.

What Do NLP Engineers Do?

1. Build & Train AI Models
   - Develop algorithms for tasks like text classification, sentiment analysis, chatbots, translation, and speech recognition.
   - Use machine learning (ML) & deep learning (DL) models (e.g., BERT, GPT, Transformers).
2. Preprocess & Analyze Text Data
   - Clean and structure text data (tokenization, stemming, lemmatization).
   - Work with large datasets (e.g., social media posts, customer reviews, books).
3. Deploy NLP Solutions
   - Integrate models into real-world applications (e.g., virtual assistants like Siri/Alexa, spam filters, auto-correct tools).
4. Optimize Performance
   - Fine-tune models for speed, accuracy, and efficiency.
   - Work with cloud platforms like AWS, Google Cloud, or Azure.

Skills Needed to Become an NLP Engineer

- Programming: Python (key libraries: NLTK, spaCy, Hugging Face, TensorFlow/PyTorch).
- Machine Learning: Understanding of ML algorithms (RNNs, LSTMs, Transformers).
- Linguistics Basics: Knowledge of syntax, semantics, and grammar.
- Math & Stats: Probability, linear algebra, calculus.
- Data Handling: SQL, Pandas, NumPy.
- Software Engineering: APIs, Docker, cloud computing.

How to Start as a Student?

1. Learn Python & ML Basics (Coursera, Udemy, freeCodeCamp).
2. Take NLP Courses (Stanford's NLP, Hugging Face tutorials).
3. Work on Projects (Build a chatbot, sentiment analyzer, or text summarizer).
4. Internships & Research (Look for AI/NLP roles in startups or labs).
5. Join NLP Communities (Kaggle, GitHub, arXiv for research papers).

Career Opportunities

- Job Roles: NLP Engineer, AI Researcher, Data Scientist (NLP focus), Computational Linguist.
- Industries: Tech (Google, OpenAI), Healthcare, Finance, E-commerce, Academia.

Salary: $74,000 to $150,000 Annually

Timeline of Certification: 25 to 40 hours of required study time-four to five hours per day or four weeks consecutively

59 Computer Vision Engineer

A Computer Vision Engineer is a specialized professional who develops algorithms and systems that enable computers to interpret and understand visual data from the world, such as images and videos. They work at the intersection of artificial intelligence (AI), machine learning (ML), and image processing to create applications like facial recognition, self-driving cars, medical image analysis, and augmented reality.

Key Responsibilities of a Computer Vision Engineer:

1. Developing & Training Models – Building deep learning models (using frameworks like TensorFlow, PyTorch) for object detection, segmentation, and classification.
2. Image/Video Processing – Enhancing and preprocessing visual data for better model performance.
3. Algorithm Optimization – Improving speed and accuracy of vision systems for real-time applications.
4. Deployment – Integrating models into production systems (e.g., cloud, edge devices like drones or smartphones).
5. Research – Staying updated with the latest advancements (e.g., CNNs, Transformers, GANs).

Skills Required:

- Programming: Python (most common), C++, MATLAB
- Libraries/Frameworks: OpenCV, TensorFlow, PyTorch, Keras
- Mathematics: Linear algebra, calculus, probability
- Machine Learning: Neural networks, CNN, YOLO, R-CNN
- Tools: Docker, CUDA (for GPU acceleration), cloud platforms (AWS, GCP)

Career Path for a Student:

1. Learn Fundamentals:
   - Take courses in Python, linear algebra, and ML (Coursera, Udemy, or university courses).
   - Study OpenCV and deep learning for computer vision.
2. Build Projects:
   - Face detection, license plate recognition, pose estimation, etc.
   - Use Kaggle datasets or create your own.

3. Internships & Research:
   o Join AI labs, contribute to open-source projects, or intern at tech companies.
4. Advanced Studies (Optional):
   o Pursue a master's or PhD if interested in cutting-edge research.

Job Opportunities:

- Tech companies (Google, NVIDIA, Tesla)
- Robotics & autonomous vehicles
- Healthcare (medical imaging)
- AR/VR, surveillance, and more

Salary: $111,000 to $173,000 Annually

Timeline of Certification: 25 to 40 hours of required study time-four to five hours per day or four weeks consecutively

60 MLOps Engineer

As a student, you might be exploring different career paths in tech, and MLOps Engineer is one of the most exciting and in-demand roles in the field of Artificial Intelligence (AI) and Machine Learning (ML).

What is an MLOps Engineer?

MLOps (Machine Learning Operations) is a set of practices that combines Machine Learning, DevOps, and Data Engineering to deploy, monitor, and maintain ML models in production efficiently.

An MLOps Engineer is responsible for bridging the gap between Data Science and Software Engineering, ensuring that ML models are scalable, reliable, and performant in real-world applications.

Key Responsibilities of an MLOps Engineer

1. Model Deployment – Taking ML models from research (Jupyter Notebooks) to production (APIs, microservices).
2. CI/CD for ML – Automating testing, training, and deployment of models (like GitHub Actions, Jenkins).
3. Monitoring & Logging – Tracking model performance, data drift, and system health (using tools like Prometheus, MLflow).
4. Infrastructure Management – Setting up cloud (AWS/GCP/Azure) or on-prem systems for ML workloads.
5. Scalability & Optimization – Ensuring models run efficiently using Kubernetes, Docker, and model optimization techniques.
6. Collaboration – Working with Data Scientists, Software Engineers, and DevOps teams.

Skills Required to Become an MLOps Engineer

Category	Skills/Tools
Programming	Python, Bash, PySpark
ML Frameworks	TensorFlow, PyTorch, Scikit-learn
DevOps & Cloud	Docker, Kubernetes, Terraform, AWS/GCP/Azure
MLOps Tools	MLflow, Kubeflow, TFX, Airflow
CI/CD & Monitoring	GitHub Actions, Jenkins, Prometheus, Grafana
Data Engineering	SQL, Apache Spark, Data Pipelines

How to Start as a Student?

1. Learn Python & ML Basics – Take courses on ML (Andrew Ng's Coursera course is great).
2. Explore DevOps & Cloud – Learn Docker, Kubernetes, and a cloud platform (AWS/GCP).
3. Work on Projects – Deploy a simple ML model using Flask/FastAPI + Docker.
4. Experiment with MLOps Tools – Try MLflow for tracking or Kubeflow for pipelines.
5. Internships & Open Source – Contribute to MLOps projects on GitHub or apply for internships.

Career Growth & Salary

- Entry-Level MLOps Engineer: 90K–90K–120K (varies by location)
- Senior/Lead MLOps Engineer: 130K–130K–200K+
- Future Roles: AI Architect, ML Engineer, Data Engineer, or AI Product Manager.

Cybersecurity & IT Remote Jobs

61 Cybersecurity Analyst

As a student exploring career options, a Cybersecurity Analyst is a professional responsible for protecting an organization's computer systems, networks, and data from cyber threats. They play a critical role in identifying vulnerabilities, monitoring security breaches, and implementing defensive measures.

Key Responsibilities of a Cybersecurity Analyst:

1. Threat Monitoring & Detection
   - Use security tools (like SIEM—Security Information and Event Management) to detect suspicious activity.
   - Analyze logs for signs of hacking or malware.
2. Vulnerability Assessment
   - Scan systems for weaknesses (e.g., outdated software, misconfigurations).
   - Conduct penetration testing (ethical hacking) to find security gaps.
3. Incident Response
   - Investigate security breaches (e.g., ransomware, phishing attacks).
   - Contain and mitigate damage after an attack.
4. Security Implementation
   - Configure firewalls, encryption, and intrusion detection systems.
   - Ensure compliance with security standards (e.g., GDPR, HIPAA).
5. User Awareness & Training
   - Educate employees on best practices (e.g., strong passwords, avoiding scams).

Skills Needed:

- ✓ Technical Skills: Networking, OS knowledge (Windows/Linux), SIEM tools (Splunk, Wireshark), basic coding (Python, Bash).
- ✓ Analytical Skills: Ability to investigate logs and identify attack patterns.
- ✓ Certifications (Helpful for Entry-Level):
  - CompTIA Security+ (Beginner-friendly)
  - CEH (Certified Ethical Hacker) (For penetration testing)
  - CySA+ (Cybersecurity Analyst+) (Mid-level)

Career Path:

- Entry-Level: Security Analyst, SOC (Security Operations Center) Analyst
- Mid-Level: Penetration Tester, Incident Responder
- Advanced: Cybersecurity Engineer, Security Architect

Why Consider This Career?

- High Demand: Growing field with a shortage of skilled professionals.
- Good Salary: Entry-level analysts earn 60K–60K–150K (varies by location).
- Impactful Work: You protect businesses, governments, and individuals from cybercrime.

How to Start as a Student:

- Learn basics via free resources (TryHackMe, Cybrary).
- Get hands-on with CTFs (Capture The Flag challenges).
- Pursue internships in IT/Security roles.

62 Penetration Tester

A Penetration Tester (also called an Ethical Hacker or Pen Tester) is a cybersecurity professional who legally attacks computer systems, networks, or applications to find security vulnerabilities before malicious hackers can exploit them.

What Does a Penetration Tester Do?

1. Simulate Cyberattacks – They act like real hackers but with permission to test security.
2. Find Weaknesses – They identify vulnerabilities in systems, software, or networks.
3. Exploit Vulnerabilities – They attempt to break in (ethically) to prove risks exist.
4. Report Findings – They document security flaws and suggest fixes.
5. Improve Security – Help organizations strengthen defenses against real attacks.

Skills Needed to Become a Penetration Tester

- Knowledge of networking (TCP/IP, firewalls, routers)
- Understanding of operating systems (Linux, Windows)
- Familiarity with programming/scripting (Python, Bash, PowerShell)
- Experience with hacking tools (Metasploit, Burp Suite, Nmap)
- Knowledge of OWASP Top 10 (common web vulnerabilities)
- Certifications like CEH (Certified Ethical Hacker), OSCP (Offensive Security Certified Professional), or Pentest+

Why Become a Penetration Tester?

High demand & good salary (cybersecurity is growing fast!)

Exciting, hands-on work (like a legal hacker)

Helps protect companies from cybercrime

If you're interested, start learning basics of networking, security, and ethical hacking. Try platforms like Hack The Box or TryHackMe for practice!

Salary: $97,000 to $158,000 Annually

Timeline of Certification: 25 to 40 hours of required study time-four to five hours per day or four weeks consecutively

63 Security Engineer

As a student, it's great that you're exploring career options in technology! A Security Engineer is a professional responsible for protecting computer systems, networks, and data from cyber threats. They design, implement, and maintain security measures to prevent breaches, hacking, and other cyberattacks.

Key Responsibilities of a Security Engineer:

1. Network Security – Securing networks with firewalls, intrusion detection/prevention systems (IDS/IPS), and VPNs.
2. Vulnerability Management – Identifying and fixing security weaknesses in systems.
3. Penetration Testing (Ethical Hacking) – Simulating cyberattacks to find vulnerabilities before hackers do.

4. Security Monitoring – Using tools like SIEM (Security Information and Event Management) to detect threats.

5. Incident Response – Investigating and mitigating security breaches.

6. Security Policies & Compliance – Ensuring systems follow regulations like GDPR, HIPAA, or ISO 27001.

7. Encryption & Authentication – Implementing secure access controls (e.g., multi-factor authentication) and encryption methods.

Skills Needed to Become a Security Engineer:

- Technical Skills:
    - Networking (TCP/IP, DNS, firewalls)
    - Operating Systems (Linux, Windows security)
    - Programming (Python, Bash, PowerShell for automation)
    - Cloud Security (AWS, Azure, GCP)
    - Security tools (Wireshark, Metasploit, Burp Suite, Nmap)
- Soft Skills:
    - Problem-solving, analytical thinking
    - Attention to detail
    - Communication (explaining risks to non-technical teams)

How to Start as a Student?

1. Learn the Basics:
    - Take courses in cybersecurity, networking, and programming.
    - Platforms like Coursera, Udemy, Cybrary, and TryHackMe offer great resources.

2. Get Certifications (Entry-Level):
    - CompTIA Security+ (Fundamentals)
    - CEH (Certified Ethical Hacker) (For penetration testing)
    - Google Cybersecurity Certificate (Beginner-friendly)

3. Hands-On Practice:
   ○ Participate in CTF (Capture The Flag) competitions (e.g., Hack The Box, OverTheWire).
   ○ Set up a home lab using virtual machines (Kali Linux).
4. Internships & Networking:
   ○ Apply for cybersecurity internships.
   ○ Join clubs like CyberPatriot or local cybersecurity meetups.

Career Path:

You can start as a Security Analyst → Security Engineer → Security Architect or specialize in areas like Penetration Testing, Cloud Security, or Incident Response.

Salary: $98,000 to $205,000 Annually

Timeline of Certification: 25 to 40 hours of required study time-four to five hours per day or four weeks consecutively

64 SOC Analyst (Security Operations Center)

As a student, you might be exploring career options in cybersecurity. A SOC Analyst (Security Operations Center Analyst) is an entry-level to mid-level cybersecurity professional responsible for monitoring, detecting, and responding to security threats in an organization.

What Does a SOC Analyst Do?

1. Monitor Security Alerts – Uses SIEM (Security Information and Event Management) tools like Splunk, IBM QRadar, or Microsoft Sentinel to detect suspicious activity.

2. Incident Triage & Investigation – Analyzes security alerts to determine if they are real threats (true positives) or false alarms.

3. Threat Detection – Identifies malware, phishing attacks, unauthorized access, and other cyber threats.

4. Incident Response – Takes action to contain and mitigate threats, such as blocking malicious IPs or isolating infected systems.

5. Log Analysis – Reviews system, network, and application logs for anomalies.

6. Vulnerability Management – Helps identify and patch security weaknesses.

7. Reporting & Documentation – Keeps records of incidents and provides reports to higher-level security teams.

Skills Required to Become a SOC Analyst

- Technical Skills:
  - Understanding of networking (TCP/IP, firewalls, IDS/IPS)
  - Knowledge of operating systems (Windows, Linux)
  - Familiarity with SIEM tools (Splunk, ArcSight, AlienVault)
  - Basic malware analysis & threat intelligence
  - Knowledge of common attack methods (phishing, DDoS, ransomware)
- Soft Skills:
  - Analytical thinking
  - Attention to detail
  - Good communication (for reporting incidents)

How to Start as a Student?

1. Learn the Basics:
   - Take free courses on platforms like Cybrary, TryHackMe, or Coursera.

- Study CompTIA Security+ or Certified SOC Analyst (CSA) by EC-Council.

2. Hands-on Practice:
    - Use cybersecurity labs (Hack The Box, Blue Team Labs Online).
    - Set up a home lab with SIEM tools like Splunk Free or Wazuh.

3. Get Certified (Optional but Helpful):
    - CompTIA Security+ (Entry-level)
    - Certified SOC Analyst (CSA) (Specialized for SOC roles)

4. Internships & Networking:
    - Apply for SOC internships or part-time roles.
    - Join cybersecurity communities (Discord, Reddit, LinkedIn).

Career Growth Path

SOC Analyst → Senior SOC Analyst → Threat Hunter / Incident Responder → SOC Manager / Cybersecurity Engineer

Why Become a SOC Analyst?

- High demand in cybersecurity (every company needs SOC teams).
- Great entry point into cybersecurity with growth opportunities.
- Hands-on experience with real-world threats.

Salary: $98,000 to $205,000 Annually

Timeline of Certification: 25 to 40 hours of required study time-four to five hours per day or four weeks consecutively

65 Incident Response Analyst

An Incident Response Analyst is a cybersecurity professional responsible for identifying, managing, and mitigating security incidents within an organization. If you're a student interested in cybersecurity, this could be an exciting career path for you!

What Does an Incident Response Analyst Do?

1. Detects Security Incidents – Monitors systems for signs of breaches, malware, or cyberattacks.
2. Investigates Threats – Analyzes how an attack happened, what was affected, and who was responsible.
3. Contains & Eradicates Threats – Takes steps to stop an ongoing attack and remove malicious elements.
4. Recovers Systems – Restores affected systems to normal operations after an incident.
5. Documents & Reports – Keeps records of incidents and provides recommendations to prevent future attacks.
6. Improves Security Policies – Helps strengthen defenses by suggesting better security measures.

Skills Needed to Become an Incident Response Analyst

- Technical Skills:
  - Knowledge of malware analysis, forensics, and intrusion detection.
  - Familiarity with tools like SIEM (Security Information and Event Management), IDS/IPS, and EDR (Endpoint Detection & Response).
  - Understanding of networks, operating systems (Windows/Linux), and cloud security.

- Soft Skills:
  - Problem-solving under pressure.
  - Strong communication (to explain incidents to non-technical teams).
  - Analytical thinking to trace attack patterns.

How to Start as a Student?

1. Learn Cybersecurity Basics – Take courses on platforms like Cybrary, Coursera, or TryHackMe.
2. Get Certifications – Start with CompTIA Security+, then move to Certified Incident Handler (GCIH) or Certified Cybersecurity Incident Response (CSIRT).
3. Practice Hands-On – Use labs (e.g., Hack The Box, Blue Team Labs) to simulate real incidents.
4. Internships & Networking – Join cybersecurity clubs, attend conferences (DEF CON, Black Hat), and seek internships in SOC (Security Operations Center).

Career Growth

- Entry-Level: SOC Analyst → Incident Response Analyst
- Mid-Level: Senior IR Analyst → Threat Hunter
- Advanced: Incident Response Manager → CISO (Chief Information Security Officer)

Salary: $90,000 to $172,000 Annually

Timeline of Certification: 25 to 40 hours of required study time-four to five hours per day or four weeks consecutively

66 IT Auditor

As a student, you might be exploring different career paths, and IT Auditor is a great option if you're interested in technology, cybersecurity, and risk management.

What is an IT Auditor?

An IT Auditor (Information Technology Auditor) is a professional who examines an organization's IT systems, processes, and controls to ensure they are secure, efficient, and compliant with laws and regulations.

Key Responsibilities of an IT Auditor:

1. Evaluate IT Controls – Check if systems (like databases, networks, and software) are protected against cyber threats.
2. Risk Assessment – Identify vulnerabilities that could lead to data breaches or fraud.
3. Compliance Checks – Ensure the company follows laws like GDPR, SOX, HIPAA, or ISO 27001.
4. Audit Reporting – Document findings and recommend security improvements.
5. Review IT Policies – Assess if IT governance (rules & procedures) is effective.

Skills Needed to Become an IT Auditor:

- ✓ Technical Knowledge – Understanding of networks, databases, cybersecurity.
- ✓ Analytical Skills – Ability to assess risks and detect flaws.
- ✓ Attention to Detail – Spotting weaknesses in IT systems.
- ✓ Communication Skills – Explaining technical issues to non-tech people.

✓ Certifications (Helpful) – CISA (Certified Information Systems Auditor), CISSP, CIA, or CompTIA Security+.

Career Path & Opportunities:

- Industries: Banking, healthcare, tech firms, consulting (Big 4: PwC, EY, Deloitte, KPMG).
- Job Roles: IT Auditor, Cybersecurity Auditor, Compliance Analyst, Risk Consultant.
- Salary: Varies by experience & location, but generally 70K–70K–120K+ (higher in cybersecurity).

How to Start as a Student?

- Take courses in IT, cybersecurity, or accounting.
- Learn about frameworks like COBIT, NIST, ISO 27001.
- Get an internship in IT audit or risk management.
- Consider CISA certification after gaining experience.

Salary: $69,000 to $128,000 Annually

Timeline of Certification: 25 to 40 hours of required study time-four to five hours per day or four weeks consecutively

67 Network Security Engineer

As a student exploring career options, a Network Security Engineer might be an exciting path if you're interested in cybersecurity, networking, and protecting systems from cyber threats.

Who is a Network Security Engineer?

A Network Security Engineer is a cybersecurity professional responsible for designing, implementing, and maintaining security measures to protect an organization's computer networks and systems from cyberattacks, data breaches, and unauthorized access.

Key Responsibilities:

1. Design & Implement Security Measures – Configure firewalls, VPNs, intrusion detection/prevention systems (IDS/IPS), and encryption protocols.
2. Monitor & Analyze Threats – Use security tools to detect and respond to suspicious activities.
3. Vulnerability Testing – Conduct penetration testing and security audits to find weaknesses.
4. Incident Response – Investigate and mitigate security breaches.
5. Policy & Compliance – Ensure networks meet security standards (e.g., ISO 27001, NIST, GDPR).
6. Network Hardening – Secure routers, switches, and servers against attacks.

Skills Required:

- ✓ Technical Skills:
    - Networking (TCP/IP, DNS, VPN, Firewalls)
    - Cybersecurity tools (Wireshark, Nessus, Metasploit, SIEM)
    - OS knowledge (Linux, Windows)
    - Cloud security (AWS, Azure)
- ✓ Certifications (Helpful for Career Growth):
    - CompTIA Security+ (Entry-level)
    - Certified Ethical Hacker (CEH)
    - Cisco Certified Network Associate (CCNA) Security

- Certified Information Systems Security Professional (CISSP) (Advanced)
- ✓ Soft Skills:
  - Problem-solving
  - Analytical thinking
  - Communication (explaining risks to non-tech teams)

Career Path:

1. Entry-Level: Security Analyst / Network Administrator
2. Mid-Level: Network Security Engineer / Penetration Tester
3. Senior-Level: Security Architect / Cybersecurity Manager

How to Start as a Student?

- Learn networking basics (try Cisco NetAcad or free courses).
- Experiment with cybersecurity labs (e.g., TryHackMe, Hack The Box).
- Get certifications like Security+ or CEH.
- Participate in CTF (Capture The Flag) competitions.

Salary Expectations (Varies by Location & Experience):

- Entry-Level: 60,000–60,000–90,000
- Experienced: 100,000–100,000–150,000+

Why Choose This Career?

High demand (cybersecurity jobs are growing fast).
Good salary & job stability.
Constantly evolving (new challenges every day).

68 Identity & Access Management (IAM) Specialist

As a student, understanding Identity & Access Management (IAM) is important, especially in today's digital world where security and privacy are crucial. Here's a simple breakdown:

What is Identity & Access Management (IAM)?

IAM is a framework of policies and technologies that ensures the right people (users) have the right access to the right resources (systems, apps, data) at the right time—while keeping unauthorized users out.

Key Components of IAM:

1. Identity Management – Verifying who a user is (authentication).
   - Example: Username & password, biometrics (fingerprint/face scan), or multi-factor authentication (MFA).
2. Access Management – Controlling what a user can do (authorization).
   - Example: A student may access course materials but cannot modify grades.
3. User Lifecycle Management – Managing access from onboarding (joining) to offboarding (leaving).
   - Example: When a student graduates, their access to university systems is revoked.

Why is IAM Important?

- Security – Prevents hackers from stealing data.
- Compliance – Ensures organizations follow laws (like GDPR).
- Convenience – Single sign-on (SSO) lets users log in once to access multiple services (e.g., Google accounts for Gmail, Drive, etc.).

Real-World Examples of IAM:

School/University Systems – Students log in to portals (like Moodle) with their IDs to access courses.

Social Media – You log in to Instagram, but only admins can delete accounts.

Banking Apps – You authenticate with a password + OTP, but only bank staff can approve loans.

IAM Technologies You Might Encounter:

- Single Sign-On (SSO) – One login for multiple services.
- Multi-Factor Authentication (MFA) – Extra security layer (e.g., password + SMS code).
- Role-Based Access Control (RBAC) – Permissions based on roles (student vs. teacher).

Why Should You Care?

As a student, IAM protects your data (grades, emails) and ensures only you can access your accounts. Learning about IAM can also help in careers like cybersecurity, IT, or cloud computing.

Salary: $94,000 to $158,000 Annually

Timeline of Certification: 25 to 40 hours of required study time-four to five hours per day or four weeks consecutively

69 GRC Analyst (Governance, Risk, Compliance)

As a student exploring career options, a GRC Analyst (Governance, Risk, and Compliance) is a professional who helps organizations manage their regulatory requirements, mitigate risks, and ensure proper governance practices. This role is crucial in industries like finance, healthcare, cybersecurity, and technology, where compliance with laws and regulations is critical.

Key Responsibilities of a GRC Analyst:

1. Governance
   - Ensures company policies align with legal and industry standards.
   - Helps design and implement internal controls and best practices.
   - Works with leadership to maintain ethical and efficient business operations.
2. Risk Management
   - Identifies, assesses, and mitigates risks (e.g., cybersecurity, financial, operational).
   - Conducts risk assessments and recommends solutions.
   - Monitors emerging threats and compliance changes.
3. Compliance
   - Ensures the company follows laws (e.g., GDPR, HIPAA, SOX, PCI-DSS).
   - Conducts audits and prepares reports for regulators.
   - Trains employees on compliance policies.

Skills Needed for a GRC Analyst:

- Knowledge of regulatory frameworks (e.g., ISO 27001, NIST, COBIT).

- Analytical thinking to assess risks and compliance gaps.
- Communication skills to explain policies to stakeholders.
- Familiarity with GRC tools (e.g., RSA Archer, MetricStream).
- Basic understanding of cybersecurity and data privacy.

Career Path & Opportunities:

- Entry-Level: GRC Analyst → Mid-Level: GRC Consultant/ Manager → Senior-Level: Chief Risk/Compliance Officer.
- Industries: Banking, Healthcare, IT, Consulting, Government.

How to Start as a Student?

- Take courses in risk management, cybersecurity, or compliance.
- Earn certifications like CompTIA Security+, CISA, or CRISC.
- Intern in IT audit, compliance, or risk management.

This role is great if you enjoy problem-solving, regulations, and protecting organizations from risks.

Salary: $60,000 to $197,000 Annually

Timeline of Certification: 25 to 40 hours of required study time-four to five hours per day or four weeks consecutively

70 Threat Intelligence Analyst

As a student exploring career options, a Threat Intelligence Analyst might be an exciting role if you're interested in cybersecurity, investigations, and problem-solving. Here's a breakdown of what it entails:

What is a Threat Intelligence Analyst?

A Threat Intelligence Analyst is a cybersecurity professional who researches, analyzes, and tracks cyber threats (like hackers, malware, ransomware, or phishing campaigns) to help organizations defend against attacks. They gather data from various sources, interpret cybercriminal tactics, and provide actionable insights to prevent breaches.

Key Responsibilities:

1. Collect Threat Data – Monitor dark web forums, malware reports, hacker chatter, and security feeds.
2. Analyze Cyber Threats – Study attack patterns, malware behavior, and hacker techniques.
3. Produce Intelligence Reports – Summarize findings for IT teams, executives, or law enforcement.
4. Help Prevent Attacks – Recommend security improvements (firewall rules, patches, employee training).
5. Track Threat Actors – Investigate hacker groups, nation-state attackers, or cybercriminal networks.

Skills Needed:

- ✓ Technical Skills:
  - Knowledge of malware analysis, network security, and hacking techniques.
  - Familiarity with tools like SIEM (Splunk, IBM QRadar), threat feeds (MITRE ATT&CK), and OSINT (open-source intelligence).
  - Basic scripting (Python, PowerShell) for automation.
- ✓ Analytical Skills:
  - Strong research and pattern recognition abilities.
  - Ability to connect dots between different cyber incidents.

✓ Soft Skills:

- Curiosity and persistence (cyber threats evolve constantly).
- Good communication (explaining threats to non-technical teams).

How to Start as a Student:

1. Learn Cybersecurity Basics – Take free courses on platforms like Cybrary, TryHackMe, or Coursera.
2. Get Certifications – Consider entry-level certs like CompTIA Security+ or Certified Threat Intelligence Analyst (CTIA).
3. Practice Hands-On – Participate in CTF (Capture The Flag) competitions or analyze malware in safe environments.
4. Follow Threat News – Read blogs (Krebs on Security, Threatpost) and follow cybersecurity experts on Twitter.
5. Internships & Networking – Look for cybersecurity internships or join student clubs (e.g., cybersecurity clubs, hackathons).

Career Path:

Many Threat Intelligence Analysts start as SOC Analysts or Security Analysts before specializing. With experience, you could move into roles like:

- Senior Threat Intelligence Analyst
- Cyber Threat Hunter
- Security Operations Center (SOC) Manager
- Incident Responder

Why Consider This Role?

- High demand (companies need proactive threat detection).
- Combines tech skills with investigative work (like cyber detective work!).
- Salaries are strong (entry-level: 70K–70K–90K; experienced: $100K+).

Other High-Demand Remote Tech Jobs

71 Technical Writer (Cloud, DevOps, APIs, etc.)

As a student exploring career options, you might find the role of a Technical Writer (especially in domains like Cloud, DevOps, and APIs) interesting. Here's a breakdown of what it entails:

What is a Technical Writer?

A technical writer creates clear, concise, and structured documentation to help users understand complex technical topics. They bridge the gap between developers/engineers and end-users by explaining concepts in an easy-to-follow manner.

Technical Writing in Cloud, DevOps & APIs

In these domains, technical writers focus on documenting:

1. Cloud Computing (AWS, Azure, GCP)
   - User guides for cloud services
   - Tutorials on deploying applications
   - Best practices for security & cost optimization
2. DevOps & CI/CD (Docker, Kubernetes, Jenkins, Terraform)
   - Documentation for infrastructure-as-code (IaC)
   - CI/CD pipeline setup guides
   - Troubleshooting & debugging tips
3. APIs & Developer Tools
   - API reference documentation (Swagger/OpenAPI)
   - SDK guides for developers
   - Code samples & integration tutorials

Skills Required

- Strong Writing & Communication – Ability to explain complex topics simply.
- Technical Understanding – Basics of programming, cloud, and DevOps tools.
- Tools & Technologies – Markdown, Git, Swagger, Confluence, VS Code, etc.
- Research & Collaboration – Work with engineers to gather accurate info.

Why Consider This Career?

High demand in tech companies (FAANG, startups, SaaS firms).
Remote-friendly & flexible work options.
Good pay (entry-level: 60K–60K–90K; experienced: $100K+).
Continuous learning (you'll always work with new tech).

How to Start as a Student?

- Learn basics of Cloud (AWS/Azure free tier) & Git.
- Practice writing GitHub READMEs or blog posts on tech topics.
- Contribute to open-source projects (look for "docs" issues on GitHub).
- Take a technical writing course (Google, Udemy, Write the Docs).

Job Titles to Look For

- Technical Writer (Cloud/DevOps)
- API Documentation Specialist
- Developer Advocate (if you enjoy community engagement)

71 QA Automation Engineer (Selenium, Cypress)

A QA Automation Engineer (Selenium, Cypress) is a professional who specializes in automating software testing processes to ensure the quality and reliability of applications. They use tools like Selenium and Cypress to write scripts that automatically test web applications, reducing manual effort and increasing efficiency.

Key Responsibilities of a QA Automation Engineer:

1. Automated Test Development:
   - Write and maintain automated test scripts using Selenium WebDriver (Java, Python, JavaScript) or Cypress (JavaScript).
   - Automate regression, functional, and UI tests.

2. Test Framework Setup:
   - Design and implement test automation frameworks (e.g., TestNG, JUnit, Cucumber, Mocha).
   - Integrate with CI/CD pipelines (Jenkins, GitHub Actions, GitLab CI).

3. Web Application Testing:
   - Test front-end (UI) and back-end (API) components.
   - Work with REST APIs (Postman, RestAssured).

4. Defect Reporting & Analysis:
   - Identify, log, and track bugs using tools like Jira, Bugzilla.
   - Work with developers to resolve issues.

5. Performance & Cross-Browser Testing:
   - Ensure compatibility across browsers (Chrome, Firefox, Edge) using Selenium Grid or cloud tools (BrowserStack, Sauce Labs).

6. Collaboration with Teams:
   - Work with developers, manual QA, and DevOps to improve testing processes.

Skills Required:

Programming Languages:

- Java, Python, or JavaScript (Cypress uses JS).

Automation Tools:

- Selenium WebDriver (for cross-browser testing).
- Cypress (for fast, modern web testing).

Testing Frameworks:

- TestNG, JUnit, Mocha, Jest, Cucumber (BDD).

Version Control:

- Git (GitHub, GitLab, Bitbucket).

CI/CD Tools:

- Jenkins, GitHub Actions, Azure DevOps.

API Testing:

- Postman, RestAssured, Axios.

Agile/Scrum Methodologies

Why Learn Selenium & Cypress?

- Selenium is the most widely used open-source automation tool (supports multiple languages).
- Cypress is a modern, fast tool for front-end testing (easier debugging).
- High demand in the job market for automation engineers.

How to Become a QA Automation Engineer (For Students)

1. Learn Basics of Manual Testing (SDLC, Test Cases, Bug Life Cycle).
2. Learn Programming (Java/Python/JavaScript).
3. Master Selenium & Cypress (Take online courses, build projects).
4. Practice API Testing (Postman, RestAssured).
5. Work on Real Projects (GitHub portfolio helps).
6. Apply for Internships/Junior Roles.

Salary: $77,000 to $140,000 Annually

Timeline of Certification: 25 to 40 hours of required study time-four to five hours per day or four weeks consecutively

72 Product Manager (Technical)

As a student, you might be exploring different career paths, and Product Manager (Technical) – often called TPM (Technical Product Manager) – is a great role if you enjoy both technology and business.

What is a Technical Product Manager (TPM)?

A Technical Product Manager is a bridge between engineering teams and business stakeholders. They focus on the technical aspects of a product while ensuring it meets customer and business needs.

Key Responsibilities:

1. Define Technical Requirements – Work with engineers to outline how a product should be built.

2. Roadmap Planning – Decide what features to build next based on tech feasibility and business goals.

3. Work with Engineers & Stakeholders – Explain technical constraints to non-technical teams (like marketing) and business needs to developers.

4. Evaluate Tech Trade-offs – Decide between different technologies or approaches (e.g., cloud vs. on-premise).

5. Data & Metrics Analysis – Use data to measure product success and improve features.

Skills Needed:

✓ Technical Knowledge – Understanding software development, APIs, databases, cloud computing, etc. (You don't need to be an expert coder, but you should grasp tech concepts.)

✓ Product Sense – Knowing what makes a product valuable to users.

✓ Communication – Explaining tech to non-tech people and vice versa.

✓ Problem-Solving – Balancing business needs with technical limitations.

How to Become a TPM?

• Study Computer Science, Engineering, or a related field (not mandatory but helpful).

• Learn product management basics (take online courses on Coursera, Udemy).

• Gain technical exposure (learn SQL, basic coding, cloud platforms like AWS).

• Intern in product management, software development, or data analysis.

TPM vs. Normal PM vs. Engineering Manager

Role	Focus
Technical PM (TPM)	Technical side of product decisions
Product Manager (PM)	Business strategy, user needs
Engineering Manager	Manages developers, focuses on code quality

Companies Hiring TPMs:

- Tech firms (Google, Amazon, Microsoft)
- Startups (especially in AI, SaaS, FinTech)
- Big enterprises (banks, automotive, etc.)

Is TPM a Good Career for You?

If you like tech but don't want to code full-time

If you enjoy solving problems at the intersection of business & engineering

If you prefer deep coding (better suited for Software Engineering)

Salary: $83,000 to $193,000 Annually

Timeline of Certification: 25 to 40 hours of required study time-four to five hours per day or four weeks consecutively

73 UX/UI Designer (Figma, Sketch, Adobe XD)

As a student, you might be exploring career options, and UX/UI Design is a great field to consider—especially if you enjoy creativity, problem-solving, and technology.

What is a UX/UI Designer?

A UX (User Experience) Designer focuses on how a product (website, app, software) feels and how users interact with it. They research user needs, create wireframes, and test usability.

A UI (User Interface) Designer focuses on how a product looks—colors, typography, buttons, icons, and overall visual design.

Many designers work on both UX and UI, making them UX/UI Designers.

Key Tools UX/UI Designers Use

1. Figma (Popular, free for students, cloud-based, collaborative)
2. Sketch (Mac-only, great for UI design, requires plugins for prototyping)
3. Adobe XD (Part of Adobe Creative Cloud, good for prototyping & UI)

What Does a UX/UI Designer Do?

- Research (Understand user needs & behaviors)
- Wireframing (Basic layout sketches)
- Prototyping (Interactive mockups)
- UI Design (Visual styling, colors, typography)
- Usability Testing (Check if the design works well)

How to Start Learning UX/UI Design?
Learn the basics (YouTube, Coursera, Udemy)
Practice with free tools (Figma has a free plan)
Follow design trends (Dribbble, Behance)
Build a portfolio (Showcase projects, even fake ones)

Career Opportunities

- Tech Companies (Google, Apple, startups)
- Freelancing (Work remotely for clients)
- Agencies (Design & marketing firms)

Salary: $86,000 to $120,000 Annually

Timeline of Certification: 25 to 40 hours of required study time-four to five hours per day or four weeks consecutively

74 IT Support Specialist (Remote Helpdesk)

As a student, you might be exploring career options, and an IT Support Specialist (Remote Helpdesk) role could be a great fit if you enjoy technology and problem-solving. Here's a breakdown of what this job entails:

What is an IT Support Specialist (Remote Helpdesk)?

An IT Support Specialist in a remote helpdesk role provides technical assistance to users (employees or customers) from a remote location (usually from home or a non-office setting). They troubleshoot issues, guide users through solutions, and ensure smooth IT operations.

Key Responsibilities:

1. Troubleshooting – Fixing software, hardware, and network issues remotely.
2. Customer Support – Assisting users via phone, chat, email, or remote desktop tools (e.g., TeamViewer, Zoom).

3. Password Resets & Account Management – Helping users regain access to systems.
4. Software Installation & Updates – Guiding users on installing/updating programs.
5. Basic Network Support – Diagnosing Wi-Fi, VPN, or connectivity problems.
6. Documentation – Logging issues and solutions in a ticketing system (e.g., Zendesk, ServiceNow).
7. Security Awareness – Educating users on phishing scams and best practices.

Skills Needed:

✓ Technical Knowledge – Understanding of Windows/macOS, Office 365, basic networking.
✓ Problem-Solving – Ability to diagnose and fix issues efficiently.
✓ Communication – Clear and patient when helping non-tech users.
✓ Remote Tools – Familiarity with remote desktop software (e.g., AnyDesk, LogMeIn).
✓ Customer Service – Friendly and professional attitude.

Entry-Level Requirements:

• Education: A degree or certification (e.g., CompTIA A+, ITIL, Google IT Support Certificate) helps but isn't always required.
• Experience: Internships, personal tech projects, or even gaming PC troubleshooting can count!
• Soft Skills: Patience, adaptability, and willingness to learn.

Why Consider This Role?

Work from Home – Many remote helpdesk jobs offer flexibility.
Entry-Level Friendly – Great for students/new IT professionals.

Career Growth – Can lead to roles like System Admin, Network Engineer, or Cybersecurity Analyst.

How to Start as a Student?

- Get a free certification (Google IT Support on Coursera).
- Practice troubleshooting with virtual labs (TryHackMe, Hack The Box).
- Do freelance tech support (e.g., helping friends/family).
- Apply for internships or part-time remote IT jobs.

Salary: $36,000 to $55,000 Annually

Timeline of Certification: 25 to 40 hours of required study time-four to five hours per day or four weeks consecutively

75 Microsoft Certified: Azure Administrator (AZ-104)

The Microsoft Certified: Azure Administrator Associate (AZ-104) is a certification designed for IT professionals who manage and maintain Microsoft Azure cloud services. As a student, this certification can be a great way to validate your cloud administration skills and boost your career prospects in cloud computing.

What Does the AZ-104 Certification Cover?

The AZ-104 exam tests your ability to:

- Manage Azure identities and governance (Azure Active Directory, RBAC, policies)
- Implement and manage storage (Blob, File, Disk storage)

- Deploy and manage Azure compute resources (VMs, Containers, App Services)
- Configure and manage virtual networking (VNets, VPNs, NSGs, Azure Firewall)
- Monitor and maintain Azure resources (Azure Monitor, Alerts, Log Analytics)

Who Should Take AZ-104?

- Students pursuing cloud or IT careers
- IT administrators managing Azure environments
- Professionals aiming for roles like Azure Administrator, Cloud Engineer, or DevOps Engineer

Exam Details

- Exam Code: AZ-104
- Cost: ~$165 USD (varies by region)
- Format: Multiple-choice, case studies, labs
- Duration: 120 minutes
- Passing Score: ~700/1000

How to Prepare as a Student?

1. Free Learning Paths:
   - Microsoft Learn (free modules) → AZ-104 Learning Path
2. Hands-on Practice:
   - Use Azure Free Tier ($200 credit for students)
3. Study Resources:
   - Udemy, Pluralsight, Whizlabs courses
   - Practice tests (MeasureUp, ExamTopics)
4. Join Communities:
   - Reddit (r/AzureCertification), Microsoft Tech Community

Why Get AZ-104 as a Student?

Enhances employability for cloud roles

Higher salary potential (Azure Admins earn 70K–70K–120K+)

Foundation for advanced certs (AZ-305, Azure DevOps)

76 Google Professional Cloud Architect

As a student, if you're interested in cloud computing and Google Cloud Platform (GCP), the Google Professional Cloud Architect certification is a great career goal to work toward. Here's what you need to know:

What is a Google Professional Cloud Architect?

A Professional Cloud Architect is a certified expert who designs, develops, and manages scalable, secure, and reliable cloud solutions using Google Cloud Platform (GCP). This certification validates your ability to:

- Design and plan cloud infrastructure
- Manage and provision cloud solutions
- Ensure security and compliance
- Optimize business and technical processes using GCP

Why Should a Student Consider This Certification?

1. High Demand – Cloud architects are among the highest-paid roles in IT.
2. Career Growth – Google Cloud skills are widely used by top companies.
3. Hands-on Learning – GCP offers free-tier credits for students to practice.

4. Industry Recognition – Google Cloud certifications are respected globally.

How to Prepare as a Student?

1. Learn GCP Fundamentals – Start with the Google Cloud Fundamentals course (free on Coursera/Qwiklabs).
2. Get Hands-on Experience – Use Google Cloud Free Tier ($300 credit for new users).
3. Study Core Topics – Focus on:
   - Compute Engine, Kubernetes, BigQuery
   - Networking & Security (VPC, IAM)
   - Data Storage & Machine Learning
4. Take Practice Exams – Google provides sample questions.
5. Consider Associate-Level First – If you're new, try Associate Cloud Engineer before the Professional level.

Exam Details

- Cost: ~$200 (discounts may be available for students)
- Format: Multiple-choice, case-study based
- Duration: 2 hours

Next Steps for You as a Student

- Join Google Cloud Student Programs (like Google Cloud Ready Facilitator).
- Follow Google's Cloud Architect Learning Path (docs.google.com/training).
- Build projects (e.g., deploy a website on GCP, use AI APIs).

Salary: $80,000 to $200,000 Annually

Timeline of Certification: 25 to 40 hours of required study time-four to five hours per day or four weeks consecutively

77 Certified Kubernetes Administrator

A Certified Kubernetes Administrator (CKA) is someone who has passed a professional certification exam that proves they have the skills and knowledge needed to manage and operate Kubernetes clusters—the systems that run and coordinate containerized applications in the cloud.

What Is Kubernetes?

Kubernetes is an open-source platform used by many companies to automate the deployment, scaling, and management of containerized applications. It is widely used in modern cloud computing and DevOps environments.

What Does the CKA Certification Involve?

- Who Offers It: The CKA certification is offered by the Cloud Native Computing Foundation (CNCF) in collaboration with The Linux Foundation.
- Exam Format: The exam is online, proctored, and performance-based. You must solve real-world problems using the command line in a live Kubernetes environment127.
- Duration: 2 hours17.
- Number of Questions: Around 17 hands-on tasks7.
- Passing Score: Typically about 74%.
- Cost: $445 (includes one free retake).
- Validity: Certification is valid for three years7.

What Skills Are Tested?

The exam covers five main domains:

Domain	Weight
Cluster Architecture, Installation & Configuration	25%
Workloads & Scheduling	15%
Services & Networking	20%
Storage	10%
Troubleshooting	30%

You are tested on your ability to:

- Set up and configure Kubernetes clusters
- Deploy and manage applications
- Configure networking and storage
- Troubleshoot and resolve issues in clusters
- Secure and monitor Kubernetes environments

Who Should Get CKA Certified?

The CKA is ideal for:

- Students and IT professionals interested in cloud computing, DevOps, or system administration
- DevOps engineers, system administrators, and cloud engineers who want to prove their Kubernetes skills.

Why Is CKA Valuable?

- Career Boost: It demonstrates your expertise to employers and can help you stand out in the job market.

- Industry Recognition: The certification is respected by companies worldwide and is often required for roles that involve managing Kubernetes clusters.
- Practical Skills: The hands-on nature of the exam ensures you can perform real tasks, not just answer theoretical questions.

Summary

A Certified Kubernetes Administrator is someone who has proven, through a rigorous hands-on exam, that they can effectively manage Kubernetes clusters. This certification is valuable for students and professionals aiming for roles in cloud computing, DevOps, or IT operations.

Salary: $78,000 to $200,000 Annually

Timeline of Certification: 25 to 40 hours of required study time-four to five hours per day or four weeks consecutively

78 Terraform Associate (Hashicorp)

What is a Terraform Associate (HashiCorp)?

Terraform Associate is an entry-level certification offered by HashiCorp that validates your foundational skills and knowledge in using Terraform, a popular open-source tool for automating and managing cloud infrastructure using code. The certification is officially called the HashiCorp Certified: Terraform Associate.

What is Terraform?

- Terraform is a tool developed by HashiCorp that allows you to define, provision, and manage infrastructure (such as servers, databases, and networking resources) using a declarative configuration language called HCL (HashiCorp Configuration Language).
- It supports multiple cloud providers (like AWS, Azure, and Google Cloud) and enables you to automate the setup and management of complex infrastructure environments in a repeatable and consistent way.

Who is the Certification For?

- The Terraform Associate certification is designed for cloud engineers, DevOps professionals, IT specialists, or anyone interested in infrastructure automation.
- It is suitable for students and beginners who want to demonstrate their understanding of Infrastructure as Code (IaC) and Terraform basics, as well as professionals looking to formalize their skills.

What Does the Certification Cover?

The exam tests your knowledge and skills in areas such as:

- Core concepts of Infrastructure as Code (IaC)
- Understanding and using Terraform CLI (Command Line Interface)
- Writing and managing Terraform configuration files
- Managing state and remote backends
- Working with modules to create reusable infrastructure components
- Understanding Terraform workflows and lifecycle

- Differentiating between Terraform Community and Enterprise features

Exam Details

- Format: Multiple-choice questions (57–60 questions)
- Duration: 60 minutes
- Passing Score: 70% or higher
- Cost: Around $70 USD
- Validity: 2 years
- No prerequisites: Basic terminal skills and understanding of cloud infrastructure are recommended, but no prior certification is required.

Why Get Certified?

- Validates your skills in using Terraform for infrastructure automation, making you more attractive to employers in cloud, DevOps, and IT roles.
- Helps you understand and apply best practices in modern infrastructure management.
- Acts as a stepping stone for more advanced certifications and career opportunities in cloud engineering and automation.

Is it Good for Students?

- Yes. As a student, earning the Terraform Associate certification can help you stand out when applying for internships or entry-level roles in IT, DevOps, or cloud engineering10.
- Some organizations or programs may offer free or discounted exam vouchers for students10.

Summary Table

Feature	Details
Certification Name	HashiCorp Certified: Terraform Associate
Purpose	Validates foundational Terraform and IaC skills
Target Audience	Students, beginners, cloud/DevOps/IT professionals
Exam Format	57–60 multiple-choice questions, 60 minutes
Passing Score	70%
Cost	~$70 USD
Validity	2 years
Prerequisites	None (basic cloud/terminal knowledge recommended)
Benefits	Career boost, skill validation, entry to DevOps/ Cloud

In summary:

The Terraform Associate (HashiCorp) is a beginner-friendly certification that demonstrates your ability to use Terraform for automating and managing infrastructure, making it a valuable credential for students and professionals starting in cloud and DevOps fields.

Salary: $74,000 to $262,000 Annually

Timeline of Certification: 25 to 40 hours of required study time-four to five hours per day or four weeks consecutively

Other High Paying Skills

79 Copywriting

Copywriting is a professional career focused on writing words—called "copy"—that persuade people to take action, such as buying a product, signing up for a service, or engaging with a brand. As a copywriter, you create content for advertising and marketing materials like websites, emails, social media posts, brochures, billboards, and product packaging.

What Does a Copywriter Do?

- Write advertising and marketing materials (emails, ads, websites, brochures, social media posts, product packaging, and more).
- Use persuasive language to encourage readers to take action—such as making a purchase, attending an event, or signing up for a newsletter.
- Research target audiences to understand what motivates them and tailor messages accordingly6.
- Collaborate with designers, marketers, and other professionals to develop effective campaigns.

Skills and Qualities Needed

- Strong writing and communication skills.
- Creativity and the ability to think strategically.
- Understanding of marketing principles and consumer psychology.
- Ability to adapt tone and style for different brands and audiences.
- Willingness to learn about SEO (Search Engine Optimization) for online content.

Career Paths and Work Environment

- Copywriters can work as full-time employees for companies (in-house), at advertising agencies, or as freelancers/contractors with multiple clients.

- The profession offers flexibility—many copywriters work remotely and set their own schedules, especially freelancers.
- You can specialize in areas like digital marketing, direct response, social media, or technical writing.

How to Start as a Student

- You don't need a specific degree, but studying marketing, communications, or creative writing can help.
- Build a portfolio by writing sample ads, blog posts, or social media content—even if they're for imaginary brands.
- Practice writing every day and study successful ads to learn what works5.
- Take online courses or certifications in copywriting and marketing.
- Start looking for internships, freelance gigs, or entry-level jobs to gain experience.

Why Choose Copywriting?

- It combines creativity with strategy and offers the chance to make a real impact on businesses and audiences.
- Copywriting is a well-paid writing career, with opportunities for advancement and high earning potential, especially for skilled freelancers.
- The skills you learn are valuable in many industries and can lead to other roles in marketing or communications.

In summary, copywriting is about using words to connect people with products, services, or ideas they want or need. It's a creative, flexible, and in-demand profession that you can start preparing for as a student by practicing writing, learning about marketing, and building a portfolio.

Salary: $58,000 to $121,000 Annually

Timeline of Certification: 25 to 40 hours of required study time-four to five hours per day or four weeks consecutively

80 Zapier Software Engineer

As a student, you might be curious about what a Zapier Software Engineer does and what the role entails. Let me break it down for you in simple terms.

What is Zapier?

Zapier is a no-code/low-code automation platform that connects different apps (like Gmail, Slack, Trello, etc.) to automate workflows. For example, you can set up a "Zap" to automatically save Gmail attachments to Google Drive or send Slack notifications for new Trello tasks.

What Does a Zapier Software Engineer Do?

A Software Engineer at Zapier works on building, maintaining, and improving the platform. Their responsibilities may include:

1. Backend Development – Working on APIs, server logic, and database systems that power Zapier's automation.
2. Frontend Development – Improving the user interface (UI) to make it easier for non-technical users to create workflows.
3. Integrations – Developing and maintaining connections with third-party apps (like Salesforce, Shopify, etc.).

4. Scalability & Performance – Ensuring Zapier can handle millions of automated workflows efficiently.
5. Security & Reliability – Making sure user data is safe and workflows run without errors.

Skills Needed to Become a Zapier Software Engineer

- Strong programming skills (Python, JavaScript, Go, or similar languages).
- Experience with APIs and webhooks.
- Knowledge of cloud platforms (AWS, Google Cloud).
- Problem-solving skills for debugging automation issues.
- Understanding of databases (PostgreSQL, Redis).

Why Work at Zapier?

- Fully Remote – Zapier is a remote-first company.
- Impact – You help millions of users automate repetitive tasks.
- Cutting-Edge Tech – Work on a high-scale automation platform.

How Can a Student Prepare for Such a Role?

- Learn programming (Python & JavaScript are great starts).
- Build projects involving APIs (e.g., connect Twitter to Discord).
- Contribute to open-source automation tools.
- Apply for internships in SaaS or automation companies.

Salary: $126,000 to $230,000 Annually

Timeline of Certification: 25 to 40 hours of required study time-four to five hours per day or four weeks consecutive

81 | Sales Engineer

As a student exploring career options, the role of a Sales Engineer can be an exciting and lucrative profession that blends technical expertise with sales and communication skills. Here's a breakdown of what this career entails and how you can prepare for it:

What is a Sales Engineer?

A Sales Engineer (SE) is a hybrid professional who:

- ✓ Understands complex technical products/services (e.g., software, industrial machinery, cloud solutions).
- ✓ Explains technology in simple terms to customers and helps them find the best solutions.
- ✓ Works closely with sales teams to bridge the gap between technical and business needs.
- ✓ Solves customer problems by demonstrating how a product works and why it's valuable.

Key Responsibilities:

1. Technical Presentations & Demos – Showcase how a product solves a client's problem.
2. Pre-Sales Consulting – Analyze customer needs and propose solutions.
3. RFP (Request for Proposal) Responses – Help craft technical proposals.
4. Post-Sales Support – Assist with implementation and troubleshooting.
5. Relationship Building – Work with engineers, executives, and decision-makers.

Skills Needed to Succeed:

- Technical Knowledge (engineering, IT, or relevant industry expertise).
- Communication & Storytelling – Simplify complex ideas.
- Problem-Solving – Think on your feet during customer meetings.
- Negotiation & Sales Acumen – Understand pricing, objections, and closing deals.
- Collaboration – Work with sales, marketing, and R&D teams.

Industries Hiring Sales Engineers:

- Software & SaaS (e.g., Salesforce, Microsoft, cybersecurity firms)
- Industrial & Manufacturing (e.g., Siemens, GE, robotics)
- Telecom & Networking (e.g., Cisco, Ericsson)
- Energy & Green Tech (e.g., solar, EV, smart grid solutions)

How to Prepare as a Student:

1. Study a Relevant Field – Engineering, Computer Science, IT, or Business with a tech focus.
2. Develop Soft Skills – Join debate clubs, sales competitions, or Toastmasters.
3. Gain Technical Experience – Internships in tech support, pre-sales, or customer-facing roles.
4. Learn Sales Basics – Take courses in sales methodologies (e.g., SPIN Selling, Challenger Sale).
5. Get Certified – Vendor certifications (e.g., AWS, Cisco, Salesforce) boost credibility.

Why Choose This Career?

High Earning Potential – Often includes base salary + commission.

Fast Career Growth – Can move into sales management, solutions architecture, or entrepreneurship.

Exciting & Dynamic Work – Mix of travel, client meetings, and problem-solving.

Salary: $41,000 to $200,000 Annually

Timeline of Certification: 25 to 40 hours of required study time-four to five hours per day or four weeks consecutively

Blockchain Professions

82 Web3 Product Manager

As a student exploring career options, you might be curious about the role of a Web3 Product Manager (PM)—a fast-growing and exciting position in the blockchain and decentralized technology space.

What is a Web3 Product Manager?

A Web3 Product Manager oversees the development and success of products built on blockchain, decentralized applications (dApps), smart contracts, or other Web3 technologies. Unlike traditional PMs (who work on Web2 products like apps or websites), a Web3 PM must understand blockchain fundamentals, decentralized governance, tokenomics, and user behavior in a trustless environment.

Key Responsibilities of a Web3 PM:

1. Define Product Vision & Strategy
   - Align the product with Web3 values (decentralization, user ownership, transparency).
   - Decide whether the product needs a token, NFT integration, or DAO governance.
2. Understand Blockchain Tech
   - Know how different blockchains (Ethereum, Solana, Polygon, etc.) work.
   - Understand smart contracts, wallets (MetaMask, Phantom), and DeFi protocols.
3. Work with Cross-Functional Teams
   - Collaborate with developers (Solidity, Rust), designers, and community managers.
   - Bridge the gap between technical teams and non-technical stakeholders.

4. User & Community Focus
   - Web3 users are often community-driven (e.g., NFT holders, DAO voters).
   - Engage with users on Discord, Twitter, and governance forums.
5. Tokenomics & Incentive Design
   - Design systems that encourage user participation (staking, rewards, governance).
   - Avoid Ponzi-like mechanics and ensure sustainable growth.
6. Regulatory & Security Awareness
   - Navigate legal challenges (KYC, AML, securities laws).
   - Ensure smart contracts are audited to prevent hacks.

Skills Needed to Become a Web3 PM:

Blockchain Basics – Understand how wallets, transactions, and dApps work.
Product Management Fundamentals – Roadmaps, Agile, user research.
Technical Understanding – Smart contracts, APIs, Layer 2 solutions.
Community & DAO Knowledge – How decentralized governance works.
Tokenomics & Economics – Designing incentive models.

How to Start as a Student?

1. Learn Web3 Basics – Take free courses (CryptoZombies, Buildspace, Odin School).
2. Use Web3 Products – Try MetaMask, Uniswap, OpenSea, and DAO tools.
3. Join Web3 Communities – Discord, DAOs, hackathons (ETHGlobal).
4. Build a Side Project – Create a simple dApp or contribute to a DAO.
5. Intern at a Web3 Startup – Many crypto firms hire student interns.

Web3 PM vs. Traditional PM

Aspect	Web3 PM	Traditional PM (Web2)
Ownership	Users own assets (tokens, NFTs)	Company owns user data
Decision-Making	DAO voting, decentralized governance	Centralized corporate structure
Monetization	Tokenomics, gas fees, NFTs	Ads, subscriptions
Security	Smart contract risks, hacks	Data privacy concerns

Future of Web3 PM Roles

As blockchain adoption grows, demand for Web3 PMs will increase in:

- DeFi (Uniswap, Aave)
- NFTs & Gaming (OpenSea, Axie Infinity)
- DAOs & Social Networks (Friends with Benefits, Lens Protocol)

Final Advice

If you're interested, start experimenting with Web3 now—join DAOs, build small projects, and network in the space. It's a rapidly evolving field, and early experience will give you a huge advantage!

Salary: $120,000 to $300,000+ Annually

Timeline of Certification: 25 to 40 hours of required study time-four to five hours per day or four weeks consecutively

83 Computer Vision Engineer

A Computer Vision Engineer is a specialized role in the field of artificial intelligence (AI) and machine learning (ML) that focuses on enabling machines to interpret and understand visual data from the world, such as images and videos. These engineers develop algorithms and systems that can perform tasks like object detection, facial recognition, image segmentation, motion tracking, and scene reconstruction.

Key Responsibilities of a Computer Vision Engineer:

1. Algorithm Development – Designing and implementing computer vision models using deep learning (e.g., CNNs, Transformers) and traditional image processing techniques.
2. Data Processing – Collecting, cleaning, and augmenting large datasets of images/videos for training models.
3. Model Training & Optimization – Using frameworks like OpenCV, TensorFlow, PyTorch, and Keras to train and fine-tune models for accuracy and efficiency.
4. Deployment – Integrating vision models into real-world applications (e.g., robotics, autonomous vehicles, medical imaging, surveillance).
5. Performance Tuning – Optimizing models for speed and resource efficiency (e.g., edge devices, mobile apps).
6. Research & Innovation – Staying updated with the latest advancements (e.g., YOLO, Vision Transformers, GANs) and applying them to solve new problems.

Skills Required:

- Programming: Python (most common), C++, MATLAB.
- Libraries/Frameworks: OpenCV, TensorFlow, PyTorch, scikit-image.

- ML/DL Knowledge: Neural Networks, CNN, R-CNN, GANs, Transformers.
- Mathematics: Linear algebra, calculus, probability (for algorithm design).
- Tools: Docker, CUDA (for GPU acceleration), cloud platforms (AWS, GCP).
- Domain Knowledge: Image processing, 3D vision (LiDAR/SLAM), augmented reality (AR).

Industries Hiring Computer Vision Engineers:

- Autonomous Vehicles (Tesla, Waymo)
- Healthcare (Medical imaging, diagnostics)
- Robotics (Industrial automation, drones)
- Surveillance & Security (Facial recognition, anomaly detection)
- Augmented/Virtual Reality (AR/VR)
- Retail & E-commerce (Product recognition, cashier-less stores)

Career Path:

- Entry-Level: Computer Vision Engineer, ML Engineer (Vision focus)
- Mid-Level: Senior CV Engineer, Research Scientist (Vision)
- Advanced: AI/Computer Vision Lead, Principal Engineer

How to Become One?

1. Learn Python & OpenCV for basic image processing.
2. Study deep learning for vision (CNNs, object detection models like YOLO).
3. Work on projects (e.g., facial recognition, OCR, pose estimation).
4. Contribute to open-source or intern at AI-focused companies.
5. Consider advanced courses or a Master's in AI/Computer Vision.

Salary: $110,000 to $137,000+ Annually

Timeline of Certification: 25 to 40 hours of required study time-four to five hours per day or four weeks consecutively

84 DeFi (Decentralized Finance) Developer

A DeFi (Decentralized Finance) Developer is a specialized software engineer who builds financial applications on blockchain networks, eliminating intermediaries like banks. DeFi developers create smart contracts, protocols, and decentralized applications (dApps) that enable peer-to-peer financial services such as lending, borrowing, trading, and yield farming.

Key Responsibilities of a DeFi Developer:

1. Smart Contract Development
   - Write, test, and deploy secure smart contracts (mostly in Solidity for Ethereum or Rust for Solana).
   - Ensure contracts are gas-efficient and resistant to exploits (e.g., reentrancy, flash loan attacks).
2. Protocol & dApp Development
   - Build DeFi protocols like DEXs (Uniswap, PancakeSwap), lending platforms (Aave, Compound), or yield aggregators.
   - Integrate oracles (Chainlink) for real-world data.
3. Blockchain Integration
   - Work with Ethereum, Binance Smart Chain (BSC), Polygon, or Layer 2 solutions (Arbitrum, Optimism).
   - Use Web3.js or Ethers.js to interact with blockchains.

4. Security & Auditing

   o Perform security audits or use tools like Slither, MythX.

   o Follow best practices to prevent hacks (e.g., proper access control, math checks).

5. Tokenomics & Governance

   o Design token models (staking, governance tokens).

   o Implement DAO (Decentralized Autonomous Organization) voting systems.

Skills Required:

✓ Programming Languages: Solidity, Rust, Vyper, JavaScript/TypeScript.

✓ Frameworks: Hardhat, Truffle, Foundry.

✓ Tools: MetaMask, Remix IDE, Ganache.

✓ Concepts: AMMs, liquidity pools, flash loans, zk-proofs.

✓ Security: Knowledge of common vulnerabilities (e.g., sandwich attacks, MEV).

Career Path:

• Junior DeFi Dev → Smart Contract Auditor → Protocol Lead

• Opportunities in crypto startups, DAOs, or freelance gigs.

Why Become a DeFi Developer?

• High demand with lucrative salaries (100K–100K–300K+).

• Work on cutting-edge financial systems.

• Contribute to permissionless, open-source finance.

85 Blockchain Security Engineer

A Blockchain Security Engineer is a specialized cybersecurity professional focused on securing blockchain networks, decentralized applications (dApps), smart contracts, and cryptocurrency systems. Their role is crucial in preventing hacks, fraud, and vulnerabilities in blockchain-based systems.

Key Responsibilities:

1. Smart Contract Auditing
   - Reviewing and analyzing smart contracts (written in Solidity, Rust, etc.) for vulnerabilities like reentrancy, overflow, or logic flaws.
   - Using tools like Slither, MythX, or Oyente for automated scanning.

2. Penetration Testing & Vulnerability Assessment
   - Conducting security audits on blockchain protocols (e.g., Ethereum, Bitcoin, Hyperledger).
   - Simulating attacks (e.g., 51% attacks, Sybil attacks) to test network resilience.

3. Cryptography & Key Management
   - Ensuring secure implementation of cryptographic algorithms (ECDSA, SHA-256, ZK-SNARKs).
   - Protecting private keys and wallets from theft or misuse.

4. Node & Network Security
   - Securing blockchain nodes from DDoS attacks, eclipse attacks, or unauthorized access.
   - Implementing secure consensus mechanisms (PoW, PoS, BFT).

5. Incident Response & Forensics
   - Investigating blockchain exploits (e.g., flash loan attacks, rug pulls).
   - Tracing stolen funds using blockchain explorers (Etherscan, Chainalysis).

6. Compliance & Regulatory Security
   o   Ensuring adherence to security standards like NIST, ISO 27001, or SEC regulations.
   o   Implementing KYC/AML solutions for DeFi and exchanges.

Skills & Tools Required:

- Programming: Solidity, Rust, Go, Python, JavaScript.
- Security Tools: Metasploit, Burp Suite, Truffle, Hardhat.
- Blockchain Knowledge: Ethereum, Bitcoin, Polkadot, Cosmos, Layer 2 solutions.
- Cryptography: Hash functions, digital signatures, zero-knowledge proofs.
- OS & Networking: Linux, Docker, Kubernetes, understanding of P2P networks.

Career Path & Certifications:

- Certified Blockchain Security Professional (CBSP)
- Certified Ethereum Security Engineer (CESE)
- Offensive Security Certified Professional (OSCP) for blockchain pentesting

Why It's Important?

Blockchain hacks (e.g., Poly Network, DAO Hack, Ronin Bridge) have caused billions in losses. A Blockchain Security Engineer helps prevent such breaches by designing secure systems and conducting thorough audits.

Salary: $120,000 to $205,000+ Annually

Timeline of Certification: 25 to 40 hours of required study time-four to five hours per day or four weeks consecutively

86 Smart Contract Engineer

A Smart Contract Engineer is a specialized software developer who designs, builds, tests, and deploys smart contracts—self-executing programs that run on blockchain networks like Ethereum, Solana, or Polygon. These contracts automatically enforce agreements when predefined conditions are met, eliminating the need for intermediaries.

Key Responsibilities:

1. Writing Smart Contracts
   - Develop secure and efficient smart contracts in languages like Solidity (Ethereum), Rust (Solana), or Vyper.
   - Implement business logic for DeFi protocols, NFTs, DAOs, and other blockchain applications.

2. Security & Auditing
   - Prevent vulnerabilities (e.g., reentrancy, overflow) by following best practices.
   - Work with auditing firms like OpenZeppelin or CertiK to ensure contract safety.

3. Testing & Deployment
   - Use tools like Hardhat, Truffle, or Foundry for testing.
   - Deploy contracts on mainnet/testnets (Ethereum, Arbitrum, etc.).

4. Integration with dApps
   - Connect smart contracts with front-end apps using web3.js, ethers.js, or WalletConnect.
   - Work with back-end systems (oracles like Chainlink for off-chain data).

5. Optimization & Gas Efficiency
   - Reduce transaction costs by optimizing contract code.

Skills Required:

- ✓ Blockchain Fundamentals (consensus, cryptography)
- ✓ Smart Contract Languages (Solidity, Rust)
- ✓ Development Tools (Hardhat, Remix, Ganache)
- ✓ Security Practices (formal verification, audits)
- ✓ Web3 Libraries (ethers.js, web3.py)
- ✓ Understanding of DeFi/NFT Standards (ERC-20, ERC-721)

Career Path:

- Work in DeFi protocols (Uniswap, Aave), NFT projects, or blockchain startups.
- Transition into blockchain security auditing or protocol research.

Why Become One?

- High demand in the Web3 space.
- Competitive salaries (often $100K+ for experienced engineers).
- Opportunity to work on cutting-edge decentralized systems.

Salary: $110,000 to $137,000+ Annually

Timeline of Certification: 25 to 40 hours of required study time-four to five hours per day or four weeks consecutively

87 Natural Language Processing

Natural Language Processing (NLP) is a branch of Artificial Intelligence (AI) and Computational Linguistics that focuses on enabling computers to understand, interpret, and generate human language in a meaningful and useful way.

Key Aspects of NLP:

1. Text Processing & Understanding
   - Breaking down language into smaller parts (tokens, sentences).
   - Analyzing grammar (syntax) and meaning (semantics).
2. Machine Learning in NLP
   - Uses statistical models, neural networks (like Transformers), and deep learning to process language.
   - Examples: BERT, GPT, LSTM, Word2Vec.
3. Common NLP Tasks
   - Text Classification (Spam detection, Sentiment Analysis)
   - Named Entity Recognition (NER) (Identifying names, places, dates)
   - Machine Translation (Google Translate)
   - Speech Recognition (Siri, Alexa)
   - Text Generation (ChatGPT, Bard)
   - Question Answering (AI chatbots)
4. Challenges in NLP
   - Ambiguity (Words with multiple meanings)
   - Context Understanding (Sarcasm, idioms)
   - Multilingual Processing (Different languages & dialects)

Why is NLP Important?

- Powers chatbots, virtual assistants, search engines, and automated summaries.

- Used in healthcare (diagnosis from reports), finance (sentiment analysis for stocks), and customer support.

Example Workflow in NLP:

1. Tokenization → Split text into words/sentences.
2. Stopword Removal → Filter out common words (e.g., "the", "is").
3. Stemming/Lemmatization → Reduce words to base forms ("running" → "run").
4. Vectorization → Convert text to numbers (TF-IDF, Word Embeddings).
5. Model Training → Use ML/DL to analyze or generate text.

Tools & Libraries for NLP:

- Python Libraries: NLTK, spaCy, Hugging Face Transformers, Gensim.
- Frameworks: TensorFlow, PyTorch.

Salary: $110,000 to $137,000+ Annually

Timeline of Certification: 25 to 40 hours of required study time-four to five hours per day or four weeks consecutively

88 AI Software Engineer

An AI Software Engineer is a specialized role that combines software engineering with artificial intelligence (AI) and machine learning (ML) expertise. These professionals design, develop, and deploy AI-powered applications, ensuring they are scalable, efficient, and integrated into real-world systems.

Key Responsibilities of an AI Software Engineer:

1. Developing AI/ML Models
   - Implement machine learning algorithms (supervised, unsupervised, reinforcement learning).
   - Work with deep learning frameworks like TensorFlow, PyTorch, or Keras.
   - Fine-tune models for accuracy and performance.
2. Software Engineering & Integration
   - Write clean, scalable code in languages like Python, Java, or C++.
   - Build APIs (using FastAPI, Flask, or Django) to deploy AI models.
   - Optimize AI systems for speed and efficiency.
3. Data Handling & Processing
   - Work with big data tools (Spark, Hadoop) and databases (SQL/NoSQL).
   - Preprocess and clean data for training models.
4. Deployment & MLOps
   - Use Docker, Kubernetes for containerization.
   - Deploy models on cloud platforms (AWS, GCP, Azure).
   - Monitor AI systems in production (MLOps tools like MLflow, Kubeflow).
5. Collaboration & Problem-Solving
   - Work with data scientists, DevOps, and product teams.
   - Solve real-world challenges like NLP, computer vision, or recommendation systems.

Skills Required:

- ✓ Programming: Python (most common), C++, Java
- ✓ AI/ML Frameworks: TensorFlow, PyTorch, Scikit-learn
- ✓ Cloud & DevOps: AWS/GCP, Docker, CI/CD pipelines

- ✓ Math/Stats: Linear algebra, probability, calculus
- ✓ Software Engineering Best Practices: Version control (Git), testing, debugging

Career Path:

- Entry-Level: AI/ML Engineer, Software Engineer (AI focus)
- Mid-Level: Senior AI Engineer, MLOps Engineer
- Advanced: AI Architect, Research Engineer

Industries Hiring AI Software Engineers:

Tech (Google, Meta, NVIDIA)

Finance (AI-driven trading, fraud detection)

Healthcare (Medical imaging, drug discovery)

Automotive (Self-driving cars)

E-commerce (Recommendation systems)

Why Become One?

- High demand & salary (among top-paid tech roles).
- Work on cutting-edge tech (LLMs, generative AI, robotics).
- Bridge between research and real-world applications.

As a tech student, you can start by learning Python, ML basics, and cloud computing, then work on AI projects (Kaggle, GitHub)

Salary: $110,000 to $137,000+ Annually

Timeline of Certification: 25 to 40 hours of required study time-four to five hours per day or four weeks consecutively

89 Prompt Engineer

A Prompt Engineer is a specialist who designs, refines, and optimizes text-based inputs (prompts) to effectively interact with AI models, particularly Large Language Models (LLMs) like ChatGPT, Gemini, Claude, or GPT-4. Their goal is to craft prompts that generate accurate, relevant, and useful responses from AI systems.

Why is Prompt Engineering Important?

- AI models are powerful but require clear, structured instructions to produce the best results.
- Poorly written prompts can lead to irrelevant, biased, or incorrect outputs.
- Businesses use prompt engineering to automate tasks, improve chatbots, generate content, and analyze data efficiently.

Key Responsibilities of a Prompt Engineer:

1. Designing Effective Prompts – Writing clear, concise, and context-rich inputs for AI.
2. Testing & Optimization – Experimenting with different phrasings to improve AI responses.
3. Bias Mitigation – Ensuring prompts reduce harmful or biased outputs.
4. Domain-Specialized Prompts – Tailoring prompts for fields like healthcare, finance, or coding.
5. Integration with AI Systems – Working with developers to embed prompts into applications.

Skills Needed for Prompt Engineering:

- ✓ Strong Language & Writing Skills – Ability to phrase questions precisely.

- ✓ Understanding of AI Models – Knowledge of how LLMs process inputs.
- ✓ Problem-Solving & Creativity – Experimenting with different prompt styles.
- ✓ Programming Basics (Optional but Helpful) – Python, APIs, or NLP knowledge.

Examples of Prompt Engineering:

- Basic Prompt: "Explain quantum computing in simple terms."
- Advanced Prompt: *"Act as a physics professor. Explain quantum computing to a 10-year-old using analogies."*
- For Developers: "Generate Python code to scrape a website using BeautifulSoup."

Career Opportunities:

- AI/ML Companies (OpenAI, Anthropic, Google DeepMind)
- Tech Startups (Building AI-powered tools)
- Freelancing & Consulting (Helping businesses optimize AI interactions)

Final Thoughts:

As AI becomes more integral to tech, Prompt Engineering is emerging as a crucial skill—blending linguistics, psychology, and programming to "communicate" effectively with machines.

Salary: $95,000 to $270,000+ Annually

Timeline of Certification: 25 to 40 hours of required study time-four to five hours per day or four weeks consecutively

90 AI UX Designer

An AI UX Designer is a professional who designs user experiences (UX) for products or systems that use artificial intelligence (AI). Their main job is to make sure that the interaction between humans and AI-powered systems is smooth, intuitive, and meaningful.

Here's a simple breakdown of what an AI UX Designer does:

1. Understands Both AI and Human Behavior
They must understand how AI works (like machine learning, chatbots, or recommendation engines) and how people interact with technology. This helps them design interfaces where users can trust, understand, and effectively use the AI.

2. Designs User Interfaces for AI Features
They design things like:
- Smart assistants (e.g., Siri, Alexa)
- AI-driven chatbots
- Personalized content feeds
- AI-based decision-making tools (like finance or health apps)

3. Ensures Transparency and Trust
AI decisions can feel mysterious. AI UX Designers help users understand why the AI makes certain suggestions or actions, which builds trust.

4. Collaborates with Teams
They work closely with:
- AI developers (to understand the tech)
- UX researchers (to study user needs)
- Product managers (to align with business goals)

5. Focuses on Ethics and Bias

They think about fairness, data privacy, and how to avoid bias in AI systems so that the AI treats all users equally and ethically.

In short, an AI UX Designer bridges the gap between humans and intelligent machines, making complex technology easy and enjoyable to use.

Salary: $58,000 to $150,000+ Annually

Timeline of Certification: 25 to 40 hours of required study time-four to five hours per day or four weeks consecutively

91 AI Cloud Architect

An AI Cloud Architect is a technology professional who designs and manages cloud computing systems that support artificial intelligence (AI) applications. Their job is to combine knowledge of AI tools (like machine learning models, neural networks, and data processing pipelines) with cloud platforms (such as AWS, Google Cloud, or Microsoft Azure).

In simple terms:

An AI Cloud Architect helps companies build, deploy, and scale AI solutions using cloud services.

Key Responsibilities:

- Design AI cloud infrastructure: Create secure, scalable systems for AI apps.
- Select cloud services: Choose the right tools for storage, computing, and AI training.

- Support data pipelines: Make sure large amounts of data are processed efficiently.
- Deploy machine learning models: Set up systems for AI to run in the real world.
- Optimize performance: Improve speed and cost-efficiency of cloud systems.
- Ensure security and compliance: Protect data and meet legal requirements.

Skills Required:

- Knowledge of cloud platforms (AWS, Azure, GCP)
- Experience with machine learning and AI frameworks (like TensorFlow, PyTorch)
- Understanding of DevOps tools, Docker, and Kubernetes
- Programming skills (Python is very common)
- Good problem-solving and communication skills

Salary: $87,000 to $159,000+ Annually

Timeline of Certification: 25 to 40 hours of required study time-four to five hours per day or four weeks consecutively

92 Generative AI Engineer

A Generative AI Engineer is a tech professional who designs, builds, and improves AI systems that can generate new content, such as text, images, music, code, or even video. These engineers work with advanced machine learning models like GPT (for text), DALL·E (for images), and others to create tools and applications that can mimic human creativity.

Key Roles of a Generative AI Engineer:

1. Model Development:
    Train or fine-tune generative models using datasets (e.g., language models, image generators).
2. Prompt Engineering:
    Create and optimize prompts to get the best responses or outputs from AI models.
3. Tool & App Integration:
    Build applications (e.g., chatbots, content tools, design assistants) powered by generative AI.
4. Data Handling:
    Collect, clean, and prepare data for training AI systems.
5. Evaluation & Tuning:
    Test how well models perform and improve them for accuracy, relevance, or creativity.

Skills Needed:

- Programming (Python, JavaScript)
- Machine learning frameworks (like TensorFlow or PyTorch)
- Understanding of neural networks, NLP, and computer vision
- Cloud platforms (AWS, Azure, or Google Cloud)
- APIs for AI models (like OpenAI, Hugging Face)

Where Generative AI Engineers Work:

- Tech companies (Google, Microsoft, OpenAI)
- Startups building AI-powered tools
- Creative industries (gaming, film, design)
- Marketing and content automation firms

Salary: $115,000 to $159,000+ Annually

Timeline of Certification: 25 to 40 hours of required study time-four to five hours per day or four weeks consecutively

93 AI Cybersecurity Specialist

An AI Cybersecurity Specialist is a technology professional who uses artificial intelligence (AI) tools and techniques to protect computer systems, networks, and data from cyber threats like hacking, viruses, and unauthorized access.

Here's a simple breakdown of what they do:

What They Do:

- Detect Threats Automatically: They use AI systems that can spot unusual behavior or potential cyberattacks faster than humans can.
- Analyze Huge Data Sets: AI helps them scan through massive amounts of data to find patterns or signs of cyber threats.
- Prevent Attacks: AI models can predict where future attacks might happen and help put defenses in place.
- Respond to Breaches: They use AI to respond quickly and automatically to attacks, limiting the damage.
- Secure AI Systems: They also make sure that the AI systems themselves are secure and can't be tricked or hacked.

Skills Required:

- Knowledge of AI and machine learning
- Strong background in cybersecurity and network security

- Programming skills (like Python, Java, or C++)
- Understanding of data analysis and threat intelligence
- Familiarity with tools like SIEM, firewalls, intrusion detection systems, and AI libraries

Career Path:

It's a growing field, especially as AI becomes more common in both businesses and cybercrime. Many AI Cybersecurity Specialists work in tech companies, government, finance, or any organization that handles sensitive data.

Salary: $100,000 to $150,000+ Annually

Timeline of Certification: 25 to 40 hours of required study time-four to five hours per day or four weeks consecutively

94 AI in Finance Specialist

An AI in Finance Specialist is a professional who uses Artificial Intelligence (AI) tools and techniques to solve problems and create solutions in the financial industry. This specialist combines knowledge in technology, finance, and data science to help banks, investment firms, insurance companies, and fintech startups make smarter, faster, and more accurate decisions.

What They Do:

- Analyze Financial Data: Use AI to process large amounts of financial data to spot trends, risks, or opportunities.
- Develop AI Models: Create machine learning models for tasks like fraud detection, credit scoring, stock prediction, or customer behavior analysis.

- Automate Processes: Build systems that automate tasks such as trading, customer service (like chatbots), and compliance monitoring.
- Risk Management: Use AI to assess risks in investments, loans, and insurance policies more effectively.

Skills They Need:

- Programming: Python, R, or SQL.
- AI & Machine Learning: Knowledge of neural networks, decision trees, NLP, etc.
- Finance Knowledge: Understanding of markets, banking, accounting, or investment principles.
- Data Analysis: Skills in data cleaning, visualization, and interpretation.

Example Tools:

- Python libraries: Pandas, Scikit-learn, TensorFlow
- Financial tools: Bloomberg Terminal, Excel, financial APIs

Salary: $100,000 to $150,000+ Annually

Timeline of Certification: 25 to 40 hours of required study time-four to five hours per day or four weeks consecutively

95 Machine-learning product manager

A Machine Learning (ML) Product Manager is a type of product manager who specializes in creating and managing products that use machine learning technologies. Their role blends technical knowledge with product management skills to deliver intelligent systems or features.

In simple terms:

They make sure that the machine learning features (like recommendation engines, fraud detection, chatbots, etc.) are useful, usable, and deliver value to users and the business.

What They Do:

1. Understand User Needs
   - They talk to users or stakeholders to understand the problems that ML can solve.
2. Define ML Product Strategy
   - Set the vision for how ML can improve the product (e.g., "We'll use ML to recommend the best videos").
3. Work with Data Scientists & Engineers
   - Translate business needs into ML tasks.
   - Help prioritize what models to build.
   - Understand limitations of data and models.
4. Measure Model Performance
   - Decide what success looks like (accuracy, speed, fairness).
   - Track metrics like precision, recall, or F1 score.
5. Ensure Responsible AI
   - Prevent bias, ensure fairness, and make sure the product is ethical and legal.

Skills Needed:
- Basic understanding of ML concepts (like supervised learning, neural networks).
- Product management skills (roadmapping, stakeholder communication).
- Data literacy (can interpret metrics, understand data quality).
- Cross-functional collaboration (bridging the gap between tech and business).

96 Ai business analyst

An AI Business Analyst is a professional who uses artificial intelligence tools and techniques to help businesses make better decisions. Their role blends traditional business analysis with AI technologies to improve efficiency, insights, and outcomes.

Here's what they typically do:

1. Data Analysis: They work with large sets of data and use AI tools (like machine learning models or predictive analytics) to identify patterns and trends.
2. Business Problem Solving: They understand business needs and figure out how AI can solve real-world problems (e.g., reducing costs, increasing sales).
3. AI Tool Selection: They help choose the right AI tools or platforms for specific tasks.
4. Process Automation: They help companies automate repetitive tasks using AI (like chatbots, workflow automation, etc.).
5. Collaboration: They work with data scientists, engineers, and business teams to make sure AI solutions meet business goals.

In short:

An AI Business Analyst bridges the gap between technology (AI) and business strategy — helping companies use AI to grow and innovate.

Salary: $140,000 to $197,000

Study Time Required to become a Certified Professional:

97 Digital Product Developer

A Digital Product Developer is a professional who designs, builds, and maintains digital products such as software applications, websites, mobile apps, SaaS platforms, and other tech-based solutions. They combine technical skills, creativity, and problem-solving to create products that meet user needs and business goals.

Key Responsibilities of a Digital Product Developer:

1. Conceptualization & Planning
   - Works with stakeholders to define product requirements.
   - Conducts market research and user analysis.
   - Creates wireframes, prototypes, and product roadmaps.
2. Development & Coding
   - Builds the product using programming languages (e.g., JavaScript, Python, Java, etc.).
   - Works with frameworks (React, Flutter, Node.js, Django, etc.).
   - Implements databases (SQL, NoSQL) and cloud services (AWS, Azure).
3. Testing & Optimization
   - Performs debugging, unit testing, and performance tuning.
   - Ensures security, scalability, and usability.
   - Uses CI/CD pipelines for automated deployment.
4. Collaboration & Iteration
   - Works with UI/UX designers, product managers, and marketers.
   - Gathers user feedback for improvements (Agile/Scrum methodologies).
5. Maintenance & Updates
   - Monitors performance and fixes bugs post-launch.
   - Adds new features based on evolving needs.

Skills Required:

- ✓ Technical Skills: Programming, APIs, cloud computing, databases, DevOps.
- ✓ Soft Skills: Problem-solving, teamwork, communication.
- ✓ Tools: Git, Docker, Figma, Jira, analytics tools.

Career Paths:

- Frontend/Backend Developer
- Full-Stack Developer
- Mobile App Developer
- Product Manager (with experience)
- Entrepreneur (building your own digital products)

Salary: $100,000 to $180,000

Study Time Required to become a Certified Professional:

98 Fintech Developer

A FinTech Developer is a software engineer who specializes in building financial technology (FinTech) applications and systems. These developers work at the intersection of finance and technology, creating solutions that improve, automate, or disrupt traditional financial services.

Key Responsibilities of a FinTech Developer:

1. Developing Financial Applications
   - Building mobile/web apps for digital banking, payments, lending, or investment platforms.

o   Examples: Neobanks (like Revolut), payment gateways (like Stripe), or robo-advisors.

2. Working with Blockchain & Cryptocurrencies
    o   Developing smart contracts (Solidity for Ethereum).
    o   Integrating crypto wallets, exchanges, or DeFi (Decentralized Finance) protocols.

3. APIs & Integrations
    o   Connecting with banking APIs (Plaid, Open Banking).
    o   Integrating payment processors (Stripe, PayPal).

4. Security & Compliance
    o   Implementing encryption, fraud detection, and KYC (Know Your Customer) systems.
    o   Ensuring compliance with financial regulations (GDPR, PCI-DSS, AML).

5. Data & AI in Finance
    o   Using machine learning for credit scoring, fraud detection, or algorithmic trading.
    o   Analyzing big financial data for insights.

Skills Required:

- Programming Languages: Python, Java, JavaScript (Node.js), Go, or Rust.
- Blockchain: Solidity, Web3.js, Hyperledger.
- Databases: SQL (PostgreSQL), NoSQL (MongoDB), and financial data tools.
- Cloud & DevOps: AWS, Azure, Docker, Kubernetes for scalable FinTech apps.
- Security: OAuth, encryption, secure coding practices.

Career Paths:

- Payments & Digital Banking Developer
- Blockchain/Crypto Developer
- Quantitative Developer (Quant Dev) for Trading
- RegTech (Regulatory Technology) Engineer

Why Become a FinTech Developer?

- High demand due to digital banking growth.
- Competitive salaries (often higher than general software roles).
- Opportunity to work on disruptive innovations (AI finance, DeFi, CBDCs).

Salary: $129,000 to $157,000

Study Time Required to become a Certified Professional:

99 Electronic Technical Writer

An Electronics Technical Writer is a professional who creates clear, concise, and accurate documentation related to electronic products, systems, and technologies. They bridge the gap between complex technical information and end-users, engineers, or other stakeholders by producing manuals, guides, datasheets, and other instructional materials.

Key Responsibilities of an Electronics Technical Writer:

1. Writing Technical Documentation
   o User manuals, installation guides, and troubleshooting documents.

- o   Datasheets, API documentation, and white papers.
   - o   Standard Operating Procedures (SOPs) for manufacturing or testing.
2. Understanding Electronics & Engineering Concepts
   - o   Works with schematics, circuit diagrams, and PCB layouts.
   - o   Explains firmware, embedded systems, and IoT devices.
   - o   Covers topics like power electronics, signal processing, and microcontrollers.
3. Collaboration with Engineers & Developers
   - o   Gathers technical details from R&D teams.
   - o   Reviews and verifies accuracy with hardware/software engineers.
4. Use of Technical Writing Tools
   - o   Documentation tools: MadCap Flare, Adobe FrameMaker, LaTeX.
   - o   Diagramming tools: Visio, Altium (for PCB documentation), KiCad.
   - o   Version control: Git, SVN.
5. Compliance & Standardization
   - o   Ensures documents meet industry standards (ISO, IEC, IEEE).
   - o   Follows company style guides for consistency.

Skills Required:

- Strong understanding of electronics engineering concepts.
- Excellent technical writing and communication skills.
- Ability to interpret circuit diagrams, datasheets, and technical specs.
- Familiarity with embedded systems, programming (C/Python), and test equipment (oscilloscopes, multimeters).
- Knowledge of markup languages (Markdown, XML) and documentation tools.

Career Path & Opportunities:

- Work in consumer electronics, automotive, aerospace, medical devices, or IoT.
- Roles in R&D, manufacturing, or product support.
- Growth into senior technical writer, documentation manager, or technical trainer.

Why It's a Great Role for a Tech Student?

- Combines electronics knowledge with writing skills.
- High demand in tech-driven industries.
- Opportunity to learn about cutting-edge hardware/software.

Salary: $129,000 to $157,000

Study Time Required to become a Certified Professional:

100 SaaS Engineer

A SaaS Engineer (Software as a Service Engineer) is a specialized software engineer who designs, develops, deploys, and maintains cloud-based applications delivered as a service over the internet. SaaS engineers work on scalable, multi-tenant systems that serve multiple customers (tenants) from a single codebase while ensuring security, performance, and reliability.

Key Responsibilities of a SaaS Engineer:

1. Cloud-Based Development
   - Build and maintain SaaS applications using cloud platforms like AWS, Azure, or Google Cloud.

2. Multi-Tenancy Architecture
   - Design systems where a single instance serves multiple customers securely.
   - Implement tenant isolation (data separation, role-based access control).
3. Scalability & Performance Optimization
   - Ensure the application scales efficiently with increasing users.
   - Optimize databases (SQL/NoSQL), caching (Redis), and load balancing.
4. APIs & Integrations
   - Develop RESTful or GraphQL APIs for third-party integrations.
   - Work with webhooks, SDKs, and middleware for seamless connectivity.
5. Security & Compliance
   - Implement authentication (OAuth, JWT) and encryption.
   - Ensure compliance with GDPR, HIPAA, or SOC 2 standards.
6. DevOps & CI/CD
   - Automate deployments using CI/CD pipelines (GitHub Actions, Jenkins).
   - Monitor systems using tools like Prometheus, Grafana, or New Relic.
7. Subscription & Billing Systems
   - Integrate payment gateways (Stripe, PayPal).
   - Manage metered billing and usage tracking.

Skills Required for a SaaS Engineer:

- Programming: Python, JavaScript (Node.js), Java, or Go.
- Cloud Platforms: AWS (Lambda, S3, RDS), Azure, or GCP.

- Databases: PostgreSQL, MongoDB, DynamoDB.
- DevOps: Docker, Kubernetes, Terraform.
- APIs & Web Services: REST, GraphQL, gRPC.
- Security Best Practices: OWASP, IAM, encryption.

Career Path & Opportunities:

- Entry-Level: SaaS Developer → Mid-Level: SaaS Engineer → Senior-Level: SaaS Architect
- Industries: Tech startups, enterprise software, fintech, healthcare, and more.

Why Become a SaaS Engineer?

- High demand due to cloud adoption.
- Work on cutting-edge technologies.
- Solve scalability and security challenges

Salary: $129,000 to $157,000

Study Time Required to become a Certified Professional:

101 Cryptocurrency Trader

1. What is Cryptocurrency Trading?

Cryptocurrency traders buy and sell digital assets (like Bitcoin, Ethereum, etc.) to profit from price movements. Unlike long-term investors ("HODLers"), traders capitalize on short-term volatility.

2. Key Responsibilities of a Crypto Trader

- Market Analysis
  - Technical Analysis (TA): Uses charts, indicators (RSI, MACD, Bollinger Bands), and patterns to predict price movements.
  - Fundamental Analysis (FA): Evaluates news, project whitepapers, partnerships, regulations, and blockchain developments.
  - Sentiment Analysis: Tracks social media (Twitter, Reddit), whale activity, and market mood.
- Executing Trades
  - Spot Trading: Buying/selling crypto directly (e.g., Bitcoin for USD).
  - Derivatives Trading: Using futures, options, or leverage (e.g., 10x long/short positions).
  - Arbitrage: Exploiting price differences across exchanges (e.g., buying low on Binance, selling high on Coinbase).
- Risk Management
  - Sets stop-loss/take-profit orders to limit losses.
  - Diversifies portfolios to avoid overexposure to one asset.
  - Manages leverage carefully to avoid liquidation.
- Automation & Bots (Algorithmic Trading)
  - Uses Python/JavaScript to code trading bots (e.g., for arbitrage or trend-following strategies).
  - Interacts with exchange APIs (Binance, Kraken) for automated execution.

3. Tools & Skills Needed

- Exchanges: Binance, Bybit, Kraken, or decentralized exchanges (Uniswap, dYdX).

- Charting Tools: TradingView, CoinGecko, Glassnode.
- Programming (for algo-trading): Python (Pandas, CCXT library), Solidity for DeFi.
- Blockchain Knowledge: Understanding wallets (MetaMask), smart contracts, gas fees.

4. Types of Crypto Traders

- Day Trader: Closes positions within a day (high frequency).
- Swing Trader: Holds for days/weeks, riding trends.
- Scalper: Makes tiny profits from seconds/minutes trades.
- Quant Trader: Uses mathematical models for high-frequency trading.

5. Risks & Challenges

- Volatility: Prices can swing 20% in hours.
- Scams & Hacks: Rug pulls, exchange collapses (e.g., FTX).
- Regulations: Governments may ban or restrict trading.

Why It's Relevant to You as a Tech Student

- Combines coding, data science, and finance.
- Opportunities in DeFi, Web3, and blockchain startups.
- Skills in smart contracts, APIs, and automation are highly valued.

Salary: $56,000 to $300,000

Required learning and Certification is between

102 Quant Trader

Quantitative trading (quant trading) is a finance approach that uses mathematical models, algorithms, and high-speed computing to identify and execute trading opportunities in financial markets. As a tech student, you'll find it combines your technical skills with financial applications.

Core Components of Quant Trading

1. Algorithm Development: Creating mathematical models that identify trading patterns or pricing anomalies
2. Data Analysis: Processing vast amounts of market data (prices, volumes, economic indicators)
3. Backtesting: Testing strategies against historical data before live implementation
4. Execution Systems: Automated platforms that execute trades at optimal times

Technical Skills Used

- Programming (Python, C++, Java, R)
- Statistics and probability
- Machine learning/AI
- Data structures and algorithms
- High-performance computing
- Cloud computing and distributed systems

Types of Quant Strategies

1. Statistical Arbitrage: Exploiting price differences between related securities

2.   Market Making: Providing liquidity by continuously buying and selling

3.   High-Frequency Trading (HFT): Executing thousands of trades per second

4.   Machine Learning Strategies: Using AI to detect complex patterns

Salary: $120,000 to $300,000

Required learning and Certification is between

103 Salesforce Certified Administrators 1. 2. 3.

A Salesforce Certified Administrator is a professional who has demonstrated expertise in managing and optimizing Salesforce applications to support business needs. This certification validates skills in configuring, maintaining, and troubleshooting Salesforce environments. Below is an outline of key aspects of the certification:

1. Role & Responsibilities

A Salesforce Certified Administrator typically:

- Configures & Customizes Salesforce (e.g., objects, fields, page layouts, workflows).
- Manages User Access (profiles, roles, permission sets).
- Maintains Data Quality (import/export, deduplication, validation rules).
- Automates Processes (Flow, Process Builder, approval processes).
- Generates Reports & Dashboards for business insights.
- Provides User Support & Training.
- Ensures System Security & Compliance.

2. Certification Requirements

- Prerequisite: No formal requirements, but 6+ months of hands-on Salesforce admin experience is recommended.
- Exam: 60 multiple-choice/multiple-select questions (60 mins, passing score ~65%).
- Cost: $200 (plus retake fees if needed).

3. Exam Topics (2024 Syllabus)

The exam covers:

- Organization Setup (10%) – Company settings, UI customization.
- User Setup & Management (15%) – Profiles, permission sets, SSO.
- Security & Access (15%) – Object/field-level security, sharing rules.
- Sales & Marketing Apps (10%) – Leads, opportunities, campaigns.
- Service & Support Apps (10%) – Cases, knowledge base.
- Data & Analytics Management (15%) – Reports, dashboards, data tools.
- Automation (15%) – Flow, Process Builder, approval processes.
- Desktop & Mobile Configuration (5%) – Salesforce Mobile, Lightning.
- AppExchange & Integrations (5%) – App installation, basic integrations.

4. Benefits of Certification

- Career Growth: High demand for admins; average salary ~80,000–80,000–120,000 (varies by region/experience).
- Industry Recognition: Validates expertise to employers.
- Pathway to Advanced Certs: Leads to roles like Advanced Admin, Platform App Builder, or Consultant.

5. Preparation Resources

- Trailhead: Free Salesforce-admin learning paths (e.g., "Administrator Certification Prep").
- Official Study Guide: Salesforce-provided exam outline.
- Practice Tests: Focus on Force, Udemy, or Salesforce Ben mock exams.
- Hands-on Practice: Use a Developer Edition org for real-world scenarios.

6. Who Should Pursue It?

- Aspiring Salesforce professionals.
- Current admins seeking validation.
- Non-technical users transitioning into CRM roles.

Salary: Starts at $80,000 to $124,000

Time Required to study, test and become certified.

104 Market Trader 1. 2. 3.

What is a Market Day Trader?

A market day trader is someone who buys and sells financial assets (like stocks, cryptocurrencies, forex, or commodities) within the same day. The goal is to make a profit from small price changes during that day. Unlike long-term investors, day traders do not hold positions overnight.

Example:

A trader might buy a stock at $100 in the morning and sell it at $105 by the afternoon — earning a $5 profit per share.

What is Required to Master Day Trading?

To become a successful day trader, you need to build skills, gain experience, and develop discipline. Here's what's required:

1. Knowledge and Education

- Learn how markets work (stocks, crypto, forex, etc.).
- Understand technical analysis (reading charts, patterns, indicators).
- Learn risk management (how much to risk per trade).
- Know trading psychology (how to control emotions like fear and greed).

2. Tools and Technology

- A fast and reliable internet connection.
- A trading platform or app (like MetaTrader, TradingView, or Binance).
- Access to real-time market data.
- A demo account to practice before risking real money.

3. Capital

- Most traders start with some savings — even small amounts — to begin live trading.
- In stock markets, some countries require a minimum balance (e.g., $25,000 in the U.S. for pattern day trading). In crypto or forex, you can start with much less.

4. Strategy

- Use a well-tested trading strategy (e.g., scalping, momentum trading, breakout trading).
- Stick to your strategy without changing it emotionally.

5. Discipline and Practice

- Follow a daily trading routine.
- Keep a trading journal to track what works and what doesn't.
- Practice consistently and improve step by step.

Final Tip

Day trading is not a get-rich-quick scheme. Many beginners lose money at first. But with patience, education, and discipline, you can grow into a skilled trader.

How IT Remote Work as a Digital Nomad Can Help Certified Professionals Triple Their Income Using the U.S. Dollar, Euro, etc.

Page 1: Concept, Framework & Income Mechanisms

I. Introduction

- **Purpose**: Explain how certified IT professionals (e.g., AWS, Cisco, Microsoft, CompTIA, Google Cloud) can significantly increase income through remote work and geo-arbitrage.
- **Premise**: Earning in U.S. Dollars while living in lower-cost countries provides income leverage.
- **Thesis**: With strategic positioning, the right certifications, and remote contracts, IT digital nomads can **3x their income** compared to local opportunities.

II. The Power of Remote IT Work in the Global Economy

- **Global Demand for Certified IT Skills**
  - Shortage of cybersecurity, cloud, DevOps, and data professionals.
  - Remote-first hiring trend post-COVID.
- **Platforms that Power Remote Work**

- Upwork, Toptal, Freelancer, Deel, RemoteOK, FlexJobs, We Work Remotely.
- **Key Certifications in High Demand (and avg U.S. salaries):**
  - AWS Solutions Architect ($120K+)
  - CompTIA Security+ ($85K+)
  - Cisco CCNA/CCNP ($100K+)
  - Google Cloud Professional ($110K+)
  - PMP + ITIL for project managers ($90K–$120K)

III. The U.S. Dollar Advantage (Geo-Arbitrage)

- **Living in Low-Cost Countries (LCCs)**
  - Examples: Kenya, Thailand, Colombia, Mexico, Philippines.
  - Monthly living costs: $500–$1,200 vs. $4,000+ in U.S.
- **Use Case:**
  - A Kenyan AWS-certified engineer earning $4,000/month from U.S. clients.
  - Spends $800/month locally, saving $3,200.
  - Compared to a local IT job at $1,200/month—**3x earnings potential.**
- **Currency Strength & Stability**
  - The U.S. dollar retains value over time in comparison to weaker currencies (KES, THB, COP, PHP).
  - Ability to convert and save in USD via digital banks (Wise, Payoneer, Revolut).

IV. Tech Stack and Tools to Succeed as a Nomadic Remote Pro

- **Remote Productivity Tools**
  - Communication: Slack, Zoom, Teams
  - Project management: Trello, Notion, Jira, Asana
  - Coding/deployment: GitHub, GitLab, Docker, Jenkins

- **Security & Compliance**
  - Use of VPNs, multi-factor authentication (MFA), password managers (Bitwarden, 1Password)
- **Banking & Payment**
  - Use of PayPal, Wise, Deel, Remote for contract payouts
  - Multi-currency accounts for fast conversion & withdrawal

Page 2: Use Cases, Income Scaling & Strategic Roadmap

V. Income Use Cases and Case Studies

1. Freelance Engineer (AWS + Linux)

- **Earns $5,000/month via Upwork & LinkedIn clients**
- Lives in Nairobi, spends $1,000/month, saves/invests $4,000
- **3x–4x higher than local salary for same skill**

2. Remote Cybersecurity Consultant (CompTIA + CEH)

- Works with 2 U.S. clients part-time ($3,500/month combined)
- Lives in Bali, cost of living = $900/month
- Travels across Southeast Asia while working remotely

3. Cloud DevOps Engineer (Google Cloud + Terraform)

- Remote role with a Silicon Valley startup ($6,500/month)
- Lives in Medellin, Colombia ($1,200/month expenses)
- Pays taxes via treaty-friendly country setup (e.g., Panama, Estonia e-residency)

VI. Scaling Income as a Digital Nomad

- **From Freelancer to Agency Owner**
  - Outsource work locally, build a small remote team.
  - Use surplus income to train junior tech talent in LCCs.
- **Productization of Services**
  - Launch info products: eBooks, courses, toolkits, templates.
  - Income from affiliate tools (e.g., AWS, VPNs, software).

- **Invest in Dollar-Based Assets**
  - Save in USD stablecoins (USDC, USDT).
  - Use platforms like Binance, Coinbase, or DeFi apps for passive yield.

VII. U.S. Dollar Hedging & Wealth Strategy

- **Emergency Savings in USD**
  - Protects from inflation and currency depreciation.
- **Use of U.S. Fintech**
  - Digital banks (Wise, Payoneer, Mercury Bank) support global access.
- **Dual Income Streams**
  - Maintain part-time consulting while building digital assets (blog, YouTube, course).

VIII. Final Thoughts

- **Certified IT professionals are uniquely positioned** to take advantage of global remote opportunities.
- **Geo-arbitrage using the U.S. Dollar** allows a 3x income boost while improving quality of life and personal freedom.
  - **Strategic action + consistent delivery + USD payments =** financial freedom and global flexibility.

These are but limited examples of how income arbitrage can **3X** your income instantly by simply choosing to work as a digital nomad while increasing the quality of your life simultaneously. Below is a worldwide list of countries where digital nomads can thrive and 3X their US Dollar income.

1. Cape Town, South Africa

Why: Fast internet, co-working spaces, scenic beauty, and an active expat and digital nomad community.

Highlights: Table Mountain, beaches, wine country, diverse food scene.

Safety Tip: Stay in central, secure areas like Sea Point, Gardens, or Green Point.

2. Nairobi, Kenya

Why: Regional tech hub with thriving startups, many co-working spaces, and good transport links.

Highlights: Safari trips, national parks within city limits, vibrant nightlife.

Safety Tip: Stick to areas like Westlands, Kilimani, or Lavington.

3. Accra, Ghana

Why: Stable government, good expat community, growing digital economy, and friendly locals.

Highlights: Beachside living, rich culture, Afrobeat music, historical tours.

Safety Tip: East Legon and Osu are popular, safe areas.

4. Kigali, Rwanda

Why: One of Africa's safest and cleanest cities, fast-growing tech scene, and stunning scenery.

Highlights: Low corruption, eco-conscious development, and coffee culture.

Safety Tip: Kigali is widely regarded as very safe for expats.

5. Zanzibar, Tanzania

Why: Affordable island life, good internet in some hubs, and rising popularity with nomads.

Highlights: Tropical beaches, Swahili culture, historic Stone Town.

Safety Tip: Stick to tourist-friendly and well-developed areas like Paje or Nungwi.

6. Dakar, Senegal

Why: West African cultural capital with good infrastructure and artistic energy.

Highlights: Atlantic coastline, music festivals, French influence.
Safety Tip: Plateau, Almadies, and Mermoz are secure neighborhoods.

7. Windhoek, Namibia

Why: Peaceful city, reliable utilities, and access to stunning nature.
Highlights: Safari trips, German colonial architecture, desert landscapes.
Safety Tip: Windhoek is safe and quiet—ideal for focused work.

8. Essaouira, Morocco

Why: Relaxed pace of life, coastal vibe, affordable, with decent Wi-Fi in cafés.
Highlights: Windsurfing, art markets, historic medina.
Safety Tip: Very walkable and safe; smaller than Casablanca or Marrakech.

9. Victoria, Seychelles

Why: Island paradise with visa programs for digital nomads and top-tier safety.
Highlights: Beaches, marine parks, island hopping.
Safety Tip: One of the safest places in Africa with low crime rates.

10. Tofo, Mozambique

Why: Off-the-beaten-path beach town popular with adventurous nomads.
Highlights: Whale shark diving, chill vibe, surf culture.
Safety Tip: Remote but safe; stable electricity and internet in select lodges.

11. Mauritius, Africa – tropical paradise with a premium visa for remote workers.

Lisbon, Portugal
- Great weather, fast Wi-Fi, vibrant expat community.
- Digital Nomad Visa available.

Barcelona, Spain
- Creative energy, beach lifestyle, lots of co-working spaces.

Tallinn, Estonia

- First country with a digital nomad visa; modern tech-friendly infrastructure.

Tbilisi, Georgia

- Low cost of living, 1-year visa-free stay for many nationalities, friendly locals.

Berlin, Germany

- Booming startup culture, English widely spoken, solid transport.

Budapest, Hungary

- Affordable, beautiful architecture, excellent public spaces for work.

Prague, Czech Republic

- Central location in Europe, medieval charm, many remote workers.

Athens, Greece

- Ancient beauty meets a growing digital nomad scene; new visa programs.

Madeira, Portugal (Ponta do Sol)

- Launched a digital nomad village; ocean views, peaceful life.

Split, Croatia

- Coastal beauty, visa support for nomads, fast-growing tech scene.

Bali, Indonesia (Canggu/Ubud)

- Co-living spaces, spiritual vibe, popular among creatives.

Chiang Mai, Thailand

- Legendary digital nomad hotspot; cheap, safe, and chill.

Bangkok, Thailand

- Big city comforts, fast Wi-Fi, co-working cafés.

Hanoi, Vietnam

- Great street food, French colonial charm, low living costs.

Da Nang, Vietnam

- Beach city with modern infrastructure and fast internet.

Penang, Malaysia

o Multicultural, excellent food, stable internet, and affordability.

Taipei, Taiwan

o Reliable tech, strong coffee culture, friendly locals.

Tokyo, Japan

o High-tech, safe, cultural immersion for nomads with larger budgets.

Seoul, South Korea

o Ultra-fast internet, digital infrastructure, great nightlife.

Goa, India

o Laid-back lifestyle, beach cafés, vibrant international community.

From cosmopolitan cities to tropical retreats, the Americas offer diversity and modern comforts.

Medellín, Colombia

o Eternal spring climate, cost-effective, strong nomad scene.

Mexico City, Mexico

o Art, culture, and a growing number of co-working spaces.

Playa del Carmen, Mexico

o Beach lifestyle, active expat community, reliable Wi-Fi.

Buenos Aires, Argentina

o European feel, affordable living, tango and steak.

Lima, Peru

o Coastal city with good internet, delicious cuisine.

São Paulo, Brazil

o Business hub with cultural diversity and co-working spots.

Quito, Ecuador

o High-altitude charm, good weather, low cost of living.

Panama City, Panama

o U.S. dollar economy, modern skyline, stable infrastructure.

Montevideo, Uruguay
  - Quiet, safe, laid-back, and progressive.

San José, Costa Rica
  - Eco-friendly, digital nomad visa introduced, close to beaches and rainforests.

Monetary Secrets: The Hidden Truth About Money and Labor

There is an unspoken truth about money and labor recurring cycle that revolves around time, knowledge, and money. At 9:00 AM, the majority of the workforce wakes up to exchange these three currencies for wages, unknowingly fueling a system designed to benefit businesses, corporations, and government agencies.

When we work for a business, wages are deducted for taxes, which are held in a special account for one year before being paid to the IRS. During this period, companies can use those funds to expand operations, invest in inventory, or finance other ventures, as long as they eventually pay back the full tax amount due.

This raises an important question: If money is printed by the federal government, why must they collect taxes from workers? It seems illogical for a government that creates currency to demand repayment in the form of taxes.

Upon deeper reflection, the reason becomes apparent, taxes are not about funding the government but about maintaining a system that ensures control over labor and economic activity.

Businesses and institutions assign value to fiat currency, but in reality, it is labors vast productivity capacities and innovation that gives money its true worth yet is taxed heavily taxed through its use. Workers manufacture goods, build infrastructure, and provide essential services, yet they receive the smallest share of wealth while being taxed the most. Meanwhile, those in power print money at will and distribute it among the highest echelons of society while the masses suffer and struggle to survive.

This system closely mirrors historical chattel slavery, where labor was exploited for the benefit of a select few. The modern equivalent replaces chains with currency—now, the enslaving mechanism is money itself, and the enforcement agencies ensure compliance.

The IRS, Federal Reserve, and other financial institutions function as the new overseers, reinforcing economic servitude through taxation, debt, and financial penalties.

The system is not designed for financial freedom but for perpetual labor, consumption, and debt. Workers toil endlessly to earn money, only to spend it on necessities, remain in debt, and continue paying bills indefinitely.

This cycle is intentional, ensuring that the majority remain bound to a system that thrives on their labor while wealth and power concentrate at the top.

To truly understand this structure, one must compare historical systems of forced labor with modern capitalism. The parallels are undeniable— the mechanisms of control have evolved, but the fundamental structure remains unchanged.

The labor force is still at the bottom, carrying the weight of an economic hierarchy that benefits the few at the expense of the many.

Recognizing this reality is the first step toward questioning the legitimacy of the system and exploring alternatives that prioritize equity, financial independence, and true economic freedom. does it look and feel like a loop of continuous economic bondage of never-ending bills that you labor relentlessly to pay?

The Age of User-Friendly Technologies as Tools for Financial Freedom

We are now entering an era where blockchain, AI, automation, and IT-friendly technologies empower anyone willing to learn. These innovations provide a path to financial freedom, breaking the chains of fiat currency dependency and labor market constraints.

By mastering key areas—such as proof-of-stake and proof-of-work cryptocurrencies, NFTs, meme coins, AI coding, bot creation, and AI-driven trading—individuals can generate income, acquire digital assets, lend and borrow, discharge debt, and build decentralized finance (DeFi) positions that create daily wealth.

Information technology (IT) skills, such as coding, app development, peer-to-peer platforms, and software-as-a-service (SaaS) solutions, further enhance this financial liberation. When leveraged alongside cryptocurrency income streams and DeFi systems, individuals can free themselves from the grip of fiat banking, corporate control, and centralized financial structures that have long dictated economic realities in favor of financial institutions long held monopoly over access to capital.

There is no real incentive to restructure the current financial system to ensure fair and equitable access to capital for all. Therefore, an alternative must be fully embraced—cryptocurrencies, blockchain, and decentralized finance offer the solution.

Cryptocurrencies provide a diverse range of tokens and coins, often holding value equal to or greater than fiat currencies. Built on blockchain technology, they enable fast, secure transactions within seconds—far surpassing traditional banking speeds.

Additionally, decentralized finance (DeFi) empowers users with direct access to lending and borrowing while offering strategic opportunities to manage and eliminate debt. These innovative financial tools have the potential to meet the needs of many, by passing the restrictive requirements imposed by banks and other financial institutions.

The USDC token is pegged to the US dollar at a 1:1 ratio, providing a stable value. Most cryptocurrencies can be swiftly exchanged for others, making USDC a flexible bridge between fiat and crypto. Converting crypto to USDC enhances transaction fluidity, allowing users to seamlessly navigate fiat-to-crypto integrations with ease.

The advantage for cryptocurrency users is that there are no restrictions of currency conversion from crypto to any global fiat currency, furthermore cryptocurrency users can fully utilize cryptocurrency debit cards to pay bills, get cash in any currency much like a regular bank debit card. This make using cryptocurrencies even more convenient as an alternative to fiat currencies such as the USA dollar or Euro.

Currently, cryptocurrency payments can be seamlessly integrated into business operations through specialized mediation services known as cryptocurrency payment gateways.

These gateways function as intermediaries, allowing merchants to accept a wide range of digital currencies from customers and automatically convert those payments into fiat currencies such as USD, EUR, or GBP. Once the conversion is complete, the funds can be sent directly to the merchant's bank account, eliminating the need for the business to manage or hold cryptocurrencies themselves.

For example, services like CoinGate and BVNK provide platforms where merchants can accept crypto payments, have them instantly converted to fiat, and settle the proceeds into their bank accounts with minimal effort. This process typically involves the customer paying in their chosen cryptocurrency, the gateway verifying and converting the payment, and finally depositing the equivalent fiat amount into the merchant's account, streamlining the entire transaction and reducing exposure to cryptocurrency volatility

Current Options:

Most people remain oblivious to the unseen system that quietly dictates their lives—a system built for control. But blockchain, AI, automation, and DeFi present a game-changing alternative. Together, these technologies create a powerful catalyst for growth, prosperity, freedom, and true happiness.

Defi (Decentralized Finance in Action)

Earning income through DeFi is far more lucrative than traditional banking. By lending out your cryptocurrency, you can earn 5–7% on DeFi platforms, compared to the mere 0.10–0.41% APY offered by U.S. banks. DeFi also enables borrowing, lending and simultaneous debt discharge, making it a powerful and efficient financial tool for sustainable growth.

DeFi's decentralized structure stands apart by relying on cryptocurrencies instead of fiat for all transactions, eliminating the constraints of traditional tax structures and financial regulations. In contrast, fiat currencies and their banking laws reinforce the rigid boundaries of traditional finance, highlighting the stark divide between centralized systems and the borderless, unrestricted world of blockchain technology—including DeFi, cryptocurrencies, NFTs, and beyond.

The first illustration shows how the Value-to-Value end works:

- The process begins with mining Monero Token with the M2-20 Portable Mining Complex

- The next step after mining Monero, is to send your Monero from your Monero wallet to Swap Monero with a token like USDC using a swapping platform of your choice
- Then transfer your USDC to your Crypto.com Debit card
- Go Shopping

The second illustration shows how the user can generate and grow their cryptocurrency portfolio via Defi:

- This process begins with mining Monero Tokens with the M2-20 Portable Mining Complex on the PlatinumO2 Mining Pool or the utilization of Cryptocurrencies in general
- After the Monero Tokens are mined, from the Monero wallet, swap the tokens for USDC Tokens and position your USDC tokens into a reputable Defi interest earning account for the highest rate as a loan
- Next, add all interest back into account to increase the compounding amount
- You may also borrow against the loan value at a rate lower than 50% to open a second position at a good interest rate and feed all earnings into the first account.
- Then pay off the loan with earnings of the first account, then earn the income from both accounts working in tandem to continue compounding.
- In addition, earnings from mining can also be converted into USDC then added to both accounts for continuous compounding.
- The purpose of borrowing is to discharge debt while creating multiple compounding positions simultaneously.
- A rule of thumb to remember is that borrowed money is not taxable, this method fully utilizes this option.
- This method may repeated over and over again to gain the maximum compounding positions long term.

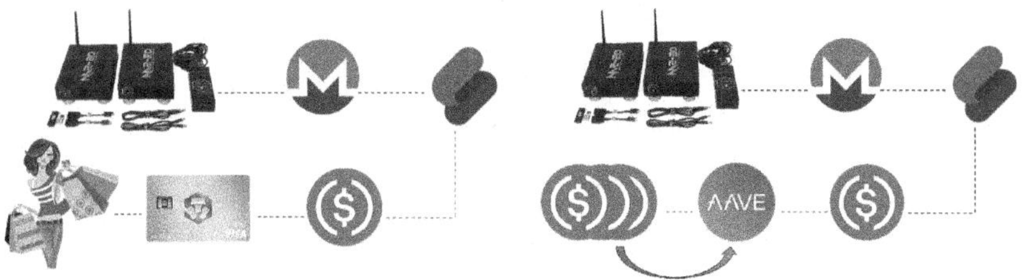

- The utilization of non-fungible tokens (NFTs) within decentralized finance (DeFi) frameworks represents a significant innovation in the evolution of digital financial systems. NFTs, traditionally associated with digital art and collectibles, are increasingly being repurposed as functional financial instruments within DeFi ecosystems. Specifically, NFTs are employed as collateral for decentralized lending, providing users with the ability to access liquidity while maintaining ownership of their underlying assets. Moreover, NFTs facilitate the tokenization of real-world assets, enabling fractional ownership and more efficient asset transfer mechanisms within blockchain environments. This integration enhances the breadth and adaptability of DeFi applications, fostering greater inclusivity and diversifying the range of accessible financial products. As DeFi continues to mature, the convergence with NFTs is anticipated to fundamentally transform conventional paradigms of asset management, lending, insurance underwriting, and financial governance, positioning NFTs as critical infrastructure components in the decentralized economy.

- The integration of artificial intelligence (AI) into decentralized finance (DeFi) systems marks a pivotal development in the trajectory of financial innovation. By leveraging advanced machine learning models, natural language processing, and predictive analytics, AI enhances the operational efficiency, security, and user experience of DeFi ecosystems. AI-driven solutions facilitate the automation of complex financial processes, optimize liquidity management, strengthen risk assessment frameworks, and enable the real-time detection and mitigation of fraudulent activities. Moreover, the incorporation of AI into smart contract execution introduces a new dimension of adaptability and precision, while AI-governed decentralized autonomous organizations (DAOs) Decentralized Autonomous Organization offer novel approaches to decentralized governance and resource allocation. As AI continues to mature within the DeFi sector, it holds the promise of fostering a more inclusive, transparent, and resilient financial infrastructure, ultimately redefining the principles of access, trust, and participation in global financial systems.

Examples of platforms that users may consider as viable Defi and Swapping options:

- 1. **Aave**
  Website: aave.com
  APY: Up to 5–15% (varies by asset and market conditions).
  Features: Lend and borrow a wide range of cryptocurrencies. Offers both stable and variable interest rates.
  Supported Assets: ETH, USDC, DAI, and more.
  Risks: Smart contract vulnerabilities and market volatility.

- 2. **Compound**
  Website: compound.finance
  APY: Up to 8–12% (varies by asset).
  Features: Algorithmic money market protocol for lending and borrowing.
  Supported Assets: ETH, USDC, DAI, and more.
  Risks: Interest rate fluctuations and smart contract risks.

- 3. **Curve Finance**
  Website: curve.fi
  APY: Up to 10–20% (varies by pool).

Features: Optimized for stablecoin trading and yield farming with low slippage.

Supported Assets: USDT, USDC, DAI, and other stablecoins.

Risks: Impermanent loss and smart contract risks.

- 4. **Yearn Finance**

  Website: yearn.finance

  APY: Up to 15–30% (varies by strategy).

  Features: Automated yield farming strategies across multiple DeFi platforms.

  Supported Assets: ETH, stablecoins, and other major tokens.

  Risks: Complex strategies and smart contract risks.

- 5. **Convex Finance**

  Website: convexfinance.com

  APY: Up to 20–40% (varies by pool).

  Features: Optimizes yield farming on Curve Finance by boosting rewards.

  Supported Assets: CRV, stablecoins, and other Curve pool tokens.

  Risks: High complexity and smart contract risks.

- 6. **Anchor Protocol** (on Terra Classic)

  Website: anchorprotocol.com

  APY: ~15–20% (historically but check current rates due to Terra's collapse in 2022).

  Features: Offers high yields on stablecoin deposits (e.g., UST).

  Supported Assets: UST (Terra USD).

  Risks: Platform instability and regulatory concerns.

- 7. **Alchemix**

  Website: alchemix.fi

  APY: Up to 10–15% (varies by asset).

  Features: Self-repaying loans and yield farming opportunities.

Supported Assets: DAI, ETH, and other major tokens.

Risks: Smart contract risks and platform complexity.

- 8. **Benqi** (on Avalanche)

  Website: benqi.fi

  APY: Up to 10–20% (varies by asset).

  Features: Lending and borrowing platform on the Avalanche network.

  Supported Assets: AVAX, USDC, and other Avalanche-based tokens.

  Risks: Network-specific risks and smart contract vulnerabilities.

- 9. **Venus Protocol** (on Binance Smart Chain)

  Website: venus.io

  APY: Up to 10–15% (varies by asset).

  Features: Lending and borrowing platform on Binance Smart Chain.

  Supported Assets: BNB, USDT, BUSD, and other BSC tokens.

  Risks: Centralization concerns and smart contract risks.

- 10. **Trader Joe** (on Avalanche)

  Website: traderjoexyz.com

  APY: Up to 20–50% (varies by pool).

  Features: Decentralized exchange and yield farming platform on Avalanche.

  Supported Assets: AVAX, JOE, and other Avalanche-based tokens.

  Risks: Impermanent loss and smart contract risks.

Key Considerations for High-Yield DeFi Platforms

- APY Variability: Interest rates can fluctuate based on market demand and platform usage.

- Risks: High yields often come with higher risks, including smart contract vulnerabilities, impermanent loss, and platform instability.

Diversification: Spread your investments across multiple platforms to reduce risk.

Gas Fees: Ethereum-based platforms may have high gas fees. Consider Layer-2 solutions or alternative chains like Avalanche or Binance Smart Chain.

Research: Always research the platform, its team, and its security audits before investing.

- How to Get Started

Choose a Platform: Select a platform that aligns with your risk tolerance and investment goals.

Connect Your Wallet: Use a Web3 wallet like MetaMask, Trust Wallet, or Coinbase Wallet.

Deposit Funds: Deposit your crypto into the platform's lending or liquidity pool.

Monitor Your Investment: Track your earnings and adjust your strategy as needed.

A Blockchain Ai Option to Labor

The contrast between trends and long-term utility is crucial for sharp discernment, providing deeper insight into tools and niche opportunities within the early stages of a trend. The use of Ai to

- **Automate Tasks** – AI can manage repetitive tasks like data entry, customer support, and scheduling.
- **Generate Content** – AI can create blog posts, social media captions, and even books.
- **Analyze Big Data** – AI can process massive amounts of data to uncover trends and insights.
- **Personalize Marketing** – AI can tailor ads, emails, and product recommendations based on user behavior.
- **Enhance Cybersecurity** – AI can detect and prevent cyber threats in real time.
- **Improve Healthcare** – AI can assist in diagnosing diseases, analyzing medical scans, and personalizing treatment plans.
- **Optimize Finance** – AI can predict market trends, detect fraud, and automate trading.
- **Advance Robotics** – AI powers robots for manufacturing, logistics, and even household tasks.
- **Boost Creativity** – AI can generate music, art, and designs based on user input.
- **Develop Smart Assistants** – AI powers virtual assistants like ChatGPT, Siri, and Alexa to help with daily tasks.
- **Healthcare** (AI for diagnosis, drug discovery, patient monitoring)
- **Finance** (AI for trading, fraud detection, risk assessment)

- **Marketing** (AI for ad targeting, content generation, customer insights)
- **E-commerce** (AI for product recommendations, chatbots, demand forecasting)
- **Cryptocurrency & DeFi** (AI for market analysis, trading bots, security)
- **Manufacturing** (AI for predictive maintenance, automation, quality control)
- **Education** (AI for personalized learning, automated grading, tutoring)

NFT (None Fungible Tokens and Redeemable NFT Tokens) NFTs (Non-Fungible Tokens) and Redeemable NFT Tokens are rapidly emerging as powerful value instruments in the digital economy. Unlike traditional cryptocurrencies, which are interchangeable, NFTs represent unique assets—whether it's digital art, music, collectibles, or exclusive access rights.

Each NFT is secured by blockchain technology, ensuring authenticity, provenance, and scarcity, all of which drive its perceived and market value. Redeemable NFTs take this concept even further by offering tangible benefits: they allow holders to exchange their digital tokens for real-world goods, services, or exclusive experiences. This fusion of digital ownership and real-world utility is redefining how we perceive and interact with value across industries.

As more creators, brands, and businesses embrace NFTs and Redeemable NFTs, they are unlocking new ways to build loyalty, create scarcity, and offer unparalleled experiences. Investors, collectors, and everyday consumers are increasingly recognizing these tokens not just as collectibles, but as strategic assets that carry real-world worth.

Whether granting VIP access to live events, limited-edition merchandise, or privileged memberships, redeemable NFTs bridge the gap between the digital and physical worlds in ways that were once unimaginable. In the evolving landscape of digital assets, NFTs and Redeemable NFTs are positioning themselves as essential instruments of value, innovation, and future economic opportunity.

This broad spectrum of options presents limitless opportunities to create, generate, and earn scalable income-yet true long-term success demands creativity, originality, and the power of boundless imagination. The key to unlocking this potential lies in a method known as the "Fourteen Principles of Creating a Niche Product or Service," which supports creativity at every stage of the process.

These principles encourage entrepreneurs and innovators to look beyond the obvious, focusing on adaptation, addition, combination, and customization to carve out a unique space in the market. For example, by adapting successful ideas from other industries, adding unique features, or personalizing products and services, creators can address unmet needs and stand out from the competition.

The process also involves making offerings easier to use, more entertaining, longer-lasting, portable, or safer-each principle providing a different lens through which to view and enhance your product or service. By systematically applying these principles, you not only foster originality and creativity but also ensure your niche is relevant, valuable, and sustainable in the long term.

One of the essential qualities of the Information Technology (IT) sector is its remarkable flexibility to work remotely. This flexibility allows professionals in most IT roles-ranging from software development and system administration to analytics and cybersecurity-to live and work from virtually any location in the world.

The rise of remote work, accelerated by technological advancements and global connectivity, has transformed the IT industry, making it possible for individuals to collaborate across time zones, access global job markets, and maintain a better work-life balance.

Employees benefit from reduced commuting costs, increased productivity, and greater autonomy over their schedules, while employers gain access to a wider talent pool and improved staff motivation and retention.

This remote work culture not only supports personal freedom and lifestyle choices but also fuels the creativity and innovation necessary to thrive in niche markets.

In summary, the path to scalable income and enduring success in today's digital economy is paved by the strategic application of niche-creation principles and the flexibility inherent in IT careers.

By embracing creativity, leveraging the "Fourteen Principles," and taking advantage of remote work opportunities, you can design a career or business that is both highly adaptive and uniquely rewarding

That is why we place such a strong emphasis on fields like Information Technology, Blockchain, Artificial Intelligence, and online entrepreneurship. These disciplines are not only at the forefront of innovation but also consistently demonstrate resilience and adaptability in the face of economic shifts.

By cultivating expertise in these areas, individuals equip themselves with the tools and knowledge necessary to thrive in a rapidly evolving digital landscape.

The demand for professionals who can navigate and leverage these technologies continues to grow, ensuring a wealth of opportunities for those who are prepared.

Mastery in these fields opens doors to diverse career paths, from software development and data analysis to decentralized finance and e-commerce ventures.

Moreover, acquiring and mastering several of these compatible professions creates a synergistic effect, amplifying one's potential for long-term financial and economic security.

The intersection of IT, Blockchain, and AI, for instance, allows entrepreneurs to innovate and solve complex problems in ways that were previously unimaginable.

Online entrepreneurship further empowers individuals to build scalable businesses with global reach, unbound by traditional limitations.

By diversifying your skill set across these high-growth sectors, you not only future-proof your career but also position yourself to capitalize on emerging trends and technologies. In an era where change is the only constant, such a proactive approach is essential for securing your future and achieving lasting success.